INSIDE
HITLER'S
BUNKER

INSIDE
HITLER'S
BUNKER

THE LAST DAYS OF THE THIRD REICH

Joachim Fest

Translated from the German by Margot Bettauer Dembo

MACMILLAN

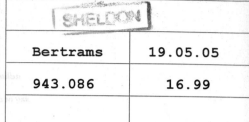

First published in Great Britain 2004 by Mac
an imprint of Pan Macmillan Ltd
Pan Macmillan, 20 New Wharf Road, Londo
Basingstoke and Oxford
Associated companies throughout the world
www.panmacmillan.com

ISBN 0 4050 4590 6

English translation first published in the United State of America
in 2004 by Farrar, Straus and Giroux LLC

9 8 7 6 5 4 3

A CIP catalogue record for this book is available from
the British Library.

Typeset by Intype London Ltd.
Printed and bound in Great Britain by
Mackays of Chatham plc, Chatham, Kent

FRONTISPIECE: Presumably the last photo taken of Hitler. He is seen standing at one of the entrances to the badly damaged Reich Chancellery alongside his longtime SS adjutant, Julius Schaub.

CONTENTS

Foreword

No catastrophe in recent history is comparable to the collapse of Germany in 1945. Never before had so many lives been lost during the fall of an empire, so many cities destroyed, entire regions devastated. Harry L. Hopkins, adviser to both American wartime presidents, was right when he drew on an image from the dawn of history, comparing the sea of ruins that was Berlin to the destruction of Carthage.

Those who lived through this time suffered more than just the inevitable terrors of a defeat exacerbated by the enormous destructive power of modern warfare. It seemed that in the death throes of Hitler's Reich a guiding force, an energy, was at work to ensure not only that Hitler's rule would end, but that the country as a whole would literally go under. From the moment he first came to power, Hitler declared again and again that he would never surrender. Early in 1945 he had assured his air force adjutant, Colonel Nicolaus von Below: "We may go down. But we will take the world down with us."

Hitler had known for a long time that the war was lost. He made remarks to that effect as far back as 1941. But he still possessed a tremendous will to destroy. Looking at those final months, one cannot possibly miss the jubilant tone that runs through all the appeals to hold out, to defend the Fatherland. It comes through, for instance, in Robert Ley's outburst after the fiery destruction of Dresden: "We [can] almost heave a sigh of relief. It is over. Now we will no longer be distracted by the monuments of German culture!" And in Goebbels's reference to "smashed prison walls" now "crushed into rubble." In the fall of 1944 and again in his "Nero command" of March 19, 1945, Hitler ordered that everything required for the maintenance of life be demolished—industrial plants and public utilities, roads, bridges, and sewage systems—so that nothing but a "desert, void of civilization" would fall into enemy hands.

He spent the last months of the war in the bunker he had ordered built in the early forties. From there, some thirty-three feet below ground, he commanded armies that had been crushed long before, and launched battles that would never take place. After seeing Hitler in one of his concrete bunkers, Claus Schenk von Stauffenberg, who tried to assassinate him on July 20, 1944, reportedly exclaimed, "Hitler in the bunker— that's the real Hitler!" Indeed the cold-bloodedness, the destructive drive, and the operatic pathos that characterized Hitler's decisions during that time were his most striking traits. Nothing gets to the root of what drove him all his life better than to examine his behavior during those weeks, when he shut himself off from the world more than ever before. Now all these traits were concentrated and intensified, shortly before everything would come to an end: his hatred of the world, his rigid adherence to old thought patterns, his tendency to think the unthinkable that enabled him for so long to pull off one success after another. But there was yet a chance to orchestrate another of those great spectacles he had always been so keen on, more grandiose than any before.

To understand what happened, one must take into account that Hitler still exercised uncontested authority in spite of the physical frailty observed by various eyewitnesses. It seems as though his aged appearance and the visible effort with which he dragged himself from room to room may even have increased his hypnotic power. In any case, scarcely anyone dared to contradict him. During the daily situation conferences, veteran generals and highly decorated officers, their faces deliberately expressionless, would gather around him in silence. Impassively they carried out the orders he issued, fully aware of how mad and senseless they were. The account that follows contains many often dismaying examples of such situations, which gave the events a uniquely theatrical quality.

Even more astonishing is the "unsteady light" that has been cast over what went on in the Führer Bunker. The phrase "unsteady light" was coined by the British historian Hugh R. Trevor-Roper, author of the first reliable account of this time, *The Last Days of Hitler,* published in 1946. Until now, no published account has managed to bring these events into sharper focus.

The question of how Hitler killed himself is a glaring example. There are at least four contradictory versions from within his closest circle. The same can be said for the whereabouts of the corpses of the dictator and the woman he had married only the night before; the "storming" of the Reich

Chancellery as claimed by the Soviet side; and many other particulars.

The uncertainty that surrounds these findings is partly due to the fact that the investigations, including those by Trevor-Roper, were begun several months after the events took place. By that time, many important witnesses had either disappeared in the postwar chaos or had been taken prisoner by the Russians and were therefore inaccessible. It wasn't until 1955, following Konrad Adenauer's trip to Moscow, that many of the SS men who had once been garrisoned in the Reich Chancellery, as well as Wehrmacht officers who had served in the Berlin battle zone, and people who had worked in the bunker, even Hitler's dentists, came back to Germany.

All at once, a number of potential sources became available—eyewitnesses to events that were unarguably the most tempestuous and momentous in German history. But opportunities to question them were squandered. For various reasons neither the events themselves nor the people who had been directly involved in them attracted much interest then.

The collapse of the Reich was certainly seen as a national catastrophe. But the nation no longer existed as such, and with the passage of time the term "catastrophe" fell victim to one of those typically German hairsplitting debates. To many, the term implied "fate," and with it a denial of guilt, as though everything that had happened had rained down from a historic thundercloud that suddenly darkened the sky. Moreover, the term did not encompass the idea of liberation, which by then had to be part of any examination of the year 1945.

This was one of the reasons behind the extraordinary indifference toward investigating and securing sources of infor-

mation related to these events. Since the 1960s only a few his-
torically aware British and American journalists have devoted
themselves to the subject and have interviewed witnesses.
Moreover, at that time historians were emphasizing a structural
approach, and—at the risk of simplification—considered social conditions more important than the events themselves.
Since then the drive to make the past come alive—the foundation of all historical studies—and the use of narrative have
been disparaged as "unscientific." At the same time, any dramatic historical material fell into disrepute, as though this kind
of representation amounted to writing "tabloid history." The
current generation of historians, attracted to microhistory,
tends to shy away from dealing with the larger and more excit-
ing picture. Yet once in a while it is necessary for the chronicler
to put aside his magnifying glass. For the way things fit together has a significance of its own and can give us information
that no mere examination of details can.

I have written this account with these considerations in
mind. The impetus came from a chapter about the Führer
Bunker that I contributed a few years ago to *Deutsche Erin-
nerungsorte* (Historic German Places), a volume compiled by
Etienne François and Hagen Schulze. In that brief essay I told
the story of the Reich Chancellery on Wilhelmstrasse and described the last day of Hitler's life. I also briefly described what
happened thereafter.

Once the book was published, a number of readers asked
for the names of books that gave a more comprehensive picture
of the collapse of the German Reich. I realized then that, except for a few works that were by now outdated in some details,
there were no books available that did justice to the monstrous

events of those final weeks and made use of the latest research. The same goes for what occurred after the curtain had fallen, when, with a bow to history's whim, a few more scenes of the bloody drama were acted out on the proscenium.

The authors whose works are listed at the end of this book have in many cases appreciably deepened my insight into the sequence of events, though a comprehensive portrayal both of what happened and important background aspects is, it seems, still needed. The present volume cannot be, and is not intended to be, more than a first step in that direction. I call it a "historical sketch," which, in four narrative chapters, tells of the turbulent events leading up to the inexorably approaching disaster. It describes what was happening in the world of the bunker as well as in the German capital as hope faded and the city went down in a maelstrom of destruction. Interspersed are four shorter reflective chapters that take their cue from these events.

Both the narrative and the reflective chapters are essential for an understanding of those fourteen days of horror. If the historian's task is to produce a slice of life as it was lived, then he must use the widest perspective possible to portray the downfall and collapse initiated by Hitler, and aided and abetted by far too many others. The Nazi leaders' completely irrational decisions—how they came about, and the fear and horror they engendered—should not be overlooked. The historian must also trace the mental and emotional tangles in which most of the actors got lost. And he should not neglect the jarring touches of comedy that only intensify the horror, to the level of a kind of infernal subzero. But in particular he should in some way communicate a sense of the sadness and mourning when reflecting on the senseless destruction that lies at the heart of this story.

A nation in extremis—that is the subject of the pages that follow, as well as the circumstances that led to its plight and that enable us to understand what happened.

INSIDE
HITLER'S
BUNKER

ONE

The Battle Begins

t 3 a.m. several flares rose into the night sky, flooding the bridgehead near Küstrin with brilliant red light. After a moment of oppressive silence a thunderous roar shook the Oder lowlands far beyond Frankfurt. As though set off by an unseen presence, sirens began to howl, telephones jangled, and books fell off shelves in places as far away as Berlin. It was April 16, 1945, the day the Soviets launched their offensive against Berlin with twenty armies, two and a half million soldiers, and more than forty thousand mortars and field guns, as well as hundreds of multibarreled Katyusha rockets—almost five hundred rocket barrels per mile. Immense pillars of fire leaped up around the villages of Letschin, Seelow, Friedersdorf, and Dolgelin, forming a wall of lightning flashes, spurting clods of earth, and flying rubble. Whole forests went up in flames, and survivors later recalled the hot windstorms that

Soviet Commander-in-Chief Marshal Georgi K. Zhukov at his command post at the start of the battle for Berlin

swept through the countryside, turning everything into fire, dust, and ashes.

After half an hour the hellish noise suddenly stopped and for a few seconds a strange stillness set in, broken only by the crackling of fire and the howling of the wind. Then the beam of a Soviet searchlight blazed straight up into the sky—the signal for 143 spotlights to be switched on. These were spaced about two hundred yards apart and were aimed horizontally across the battlefield. Their blinding beams revealed a deeply furrowed landscape, and broke up only a few miles away when they hit the Seelow Heights, that day's target for Marshal Georgi K. Zhukov, commander-in-chief of the First White Russian Front. His order initiating the battle: "The enemy must be crushed on the shortest route to Berlin. You must capture the capital of fascist Germany and raise the banner of victory over the city!"

The dramatic light show, referred to in Soviet planning circles as Zhukov's "miracle weapon," proved to be a failure and cost the Russians heavy casualties. Despite objections, Zhukov had stuck with his plan to "blind" the enemy forces, who, he believed, would already be confused and discouraged as a result of the continuing artillery fire, making them unfit to fight. Thus, in their first onslaught, the Soviets would be able to overrun the ridge, which was nearly ninety feet high and interspersed with hollows and slopes. But the dense curtain of smoke and battle haze that the heavy barrage had laid over the plain only swallowed up the beams of the searchlights, and the attackers found themselves wandering about helplessly in the murky twilight. Moreover, it turned out that the Soviet high command had completely misjudged the difficulty of the terrain, which was crisscrossed by canals, watery marshes, and drainage ditches, and was, during April, subject to springtime flooding. Troop carriers, trucks, and heavy equipment of all sorts got mired in the boggy ground, slipped deep into the mud, and had to be abandoned.

But, worst of all, just before the start of the battle, the commander of the German Army Group Vistula, General Gotthard Heinrici, who was familiar with the Russian commander's tactics, had pulled back his farthest forward defensive units, and for the most part the Soviet fire missed its target. Consequently, when the attacking Soviet infantry units—led and accompanied by massive contingents of tanks—came storming out of the billowing smoke with piercing yells and fluttering flags, the far weaker defenders, who were mostly assembled from the remnants

The generals who played a major role in the battle for Berlin. Left to right: General Vasili Ivanovich Chuikov, General Gotthard Heinrici, and General Theodor Busse

of repeatedly decimated units, merely waited till they were close enough and then shot almost randomly into the teeming shadows. At the same time hundreds of German antiaircraft guns, their barrels lowered, opened fire as soon as the outlines of the advancing tanks materialized in the diffuse light. By daybreak the onslaught had been repulsed, with the attackers sustaining heavy losses.

Zhukov's first mistake was followed by a second. Disappointed, desperate, and pressured by an angry Stalin, he decided to make a change in the previously agreed-upon strategy. He ordered his two tank armies, which had taken up positions behind the front, to go into action. Originally they were to wait until a sizable breach had been made in the German defensive line, but now they advanced to the battlefield, increasing the confusion that already reigned in the rear of the fighting troops. The tanks forced their way down clogged roads

past disoriented units, preventing a redeployment of the artillery, and cutting off the access roads for reinforcements and supplies. And since the tanks went into action without a coordinated strategy, they produced utter chaos that soon led to the complete crippling of the Soviet operation. On the evening of April 16, one of Zhukov's army commanders, General Vasili I. Chuikov, noted that the Soviet units had not carried out their assignments and had not advanced "a single step" in some places. The plan to capture Berlin on Day Five of the offensive had failed.

At Hitler's headquarters, in the deep bunker far beneath the Reich Chancellery in Berlin, the attack had been expected for several days already, with a mixture of feverish impatience and numb resignation. At first, reports of the defenders' short-lived successes once again rekindled irrational hopes of victory that were immediately fanned into unrealistic pipe dreams. Nevertheless, Hitler ordered that preparations be made for the defense of government buildings and especially the grounds around the Reich Chancellery. Antitank guns as well as mortars were to be set up, and embrasures from which to fire guns were to be created. In the afternoon he issued an "order of the day to the fighters on the Eastern Front" that invoked his genocidal mania directed at the "deadly Jewish-Bolshevik enemy," and in which he expressed his belief that the Asian onslaught would "this time too . . . bleed to death outside the capital of the German Reich. . . . You soldiers in the East know the fate that threatens German women, girls, and children," the order continued. "Old people, men, and children will be murdered, and women and girls will be forced to serve as barracks whores. The rest will be marched to Siberia."

The Red Army had reached the Oder as early as January, crossing the river in several places near Küstrin, some twenty miles north of Frankfurt-on-the-Oder. In the course of the fighting it managed to set up a bridgehead almost twenty-five miles in length and in places up to six miles deep, which threatened the entire "Nibelung Position" as far as the Neisse River. It was not until early March that the Germans responded by digging trenches in and around Berlin, erecting antitank barriers and fortified positions. But since the Soviet armies had temporarily stopped their advance, the construction of a defensive system, even a makeshift one, came to a standstill, incredible though that may seem. The work was stopped because Hitler was becoming increasingly adamant that the capital must be defended at the Oder River. No unit assigned to the front would be allowed to leave the sector. "Hold the line or perish!" was the phrase repeated in innumerable orders and directives.

Facing the Soviet forces were General Helmuth Weidling's Fifty-sixth Tank Corps and a little to the south, the Ninth Army under General Theodore Busse. General Heinrici, to whose army group both of these units belonged, had in vain pointed out the danger of encirclement should Zhukov succeed in making a breakthrough. He had also repeatedly warned that resistance could be maintained for only a short time; after that, because of the lack of experienced infantry forces, of munitions and supplies of all sorts, and especially because of the utter exhaustion of his troops, it would all be over. But Hitler's unwavering belief that sheer will could make up for any deficiencies in resources and manpower, and the grandiose but never fulfilled assurances by Göring, Dönitz, and Himmler momentarily resurrected a long-buried confidence, a confidence artificially and singlehandedly sustained by Hitler. In the end a few *Volkssturm* battalions (German territorial army units composed of very young and very old men unfit for regular duty) were taken to the front in buses to stop Zhukov's armies and motorized corps. But for some their mission was already over, even while broadcasts were still reporting that "thousands of Berliners marched to the front with their units." Russian fighter planes, which controlled the airspace over the city and its environs, had located several of the columns of vehicles en route and destroyed them in a few low-flying sorties.

Heinrici's predictions were coming true. Zhukov, having once more re-formed his units, ordered them to renew the attack when darkness fell. He was deploying his troops ever more recklessly because he had learned that his rival on the southern part of the front, Marshal Ivan S. Konev, had apparently been more successful in his maneuvers. Not only had Konev managed to cross the Neisse River at more than 130 places, thereby achieving a decisive breakthrough, but he now believed that he had ample justification for his often-repeated demand to participate in the conquest of Berlin and at the last moment to compete for the victory trophy promised to Zhukov. A silent race began, cunningly encouraged by Stalin, who made disparaging insinuations about Zhukov, now in disfavor. When Konev asked the dictator for permission to wheel about and move his right wing north through Lübben and Luckenwalde, hoping within a few days to reach the Berlin city line near Zossen, Stalin asked him if he knew that "Wehrmacht headquarters" were in Zossen. After Konev's terse "Yes," Stalin said, "Good. I approve. Have the two tank armies advance on Berlin."

Farther north, in the central sector of the Oder front, Zhukov's troops had finally reached the first houses of Seelow toward midnight. For some time a battle raged for the horseshoe-shaped ridge. In several places the German defenders—Wehrmacht units often pieced together with reserves from here and there—were outnumbered ten to one. Weak with exhaustion, they were rapidly disintegrating. In addition, Heinrici became increasingly concerned that Konev's advancing units would suddenly turn up at his rear and encircle the Ninth Army. When news reached him the next day that one of his elite units, the paratrooper division deployed on the Seelow Heights, had panicked and fled, he called the Führer Bunker.

But, as had happened several times before, his urgent proposals met with complete incomprehension. His suggestion to withdraw the troops from the Frankfurt-on-the-Oder stronghold and throw them into one of the mile-wide gaps in the defensive line was flatly rejected. And later, when he asked General Hans Krebs, who had only recently been appointed chief of staff, for permission to pull back his own units, all he could hear at the other end of the line was Krebs's labored breathing. Finally Krebs said, "Hitler will never agree to that. Maintain all positions."

By April 19 the range of hills from Seelow up to Wriezen was in Russian hands, and the area—almost a hundred years earlier, it had reminded one traveler of "distant wonderlands, all peace, color, mists"—had been transformed into a stark, dreary world of shell craters. Battling from the trenches, and taking heavy casualties, the remnants of the German defenses were collapsing section by section. According to Soviet reports, the battle had cost them more than thirty thousand lives— more credible estimates raise the number to seventy thousand— as opposed to twelve thousand casualties for the German side. But now Berlin lay scarcely forty-three miles away and the route to the capital was no longer defended by a cohesive front. Only single units were protecting several military bases and some villages, stretches of forest, and small hills. Two days later the first Soviet shells, fired from hastily positioned long-range guns, landed on Berlin's Hermannplatz amid unsuspecting pedestrians and shoppers lined up in front of the Karstadt department store, causing a gruesome bloodbath.

Less than a week before, American forces in the west had reached the Elbe River at Barby and had stopped there. Berlin was no longer a military target, the Allied Supreme Commander-in-Chief, General Dwight D. Eisenhower, had told his dumb-founded colleagues. The city belonged to the Russians; that was the agreement, and therefore the war in the northern part

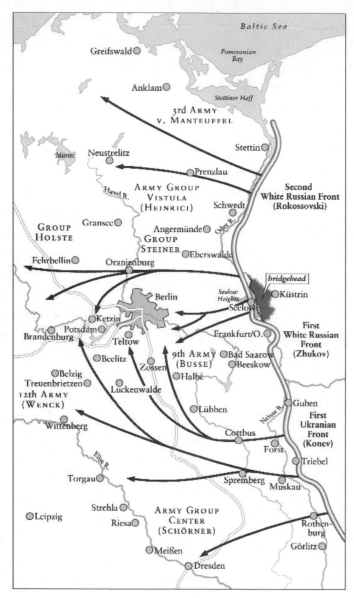

Map showing military positions at the beginning of the Russian offensive against Berlin on April 16, 1945. The Red Army had already reached the Oder River in January and established a bridgehead near Küstrin, twenty-five miles long and six miles deep in some places.

of the Reich was over for them. At the same time Field Marshal Walter Model, having previously rejected several offers to surrender, had ended the battle for the Ruhr pocket and dissolved his army group. More than 300,000 German soldiers and thirty generals were captured. Model turned to his chief of staff and asked, "Have we done all we can to justify our conduct in the eyes of world history? Is there something else we should do?" And after briefly gazing off into space, he added, "In the old days defeated generals took poison." Shortly thereafter he followed their example.

For weeks Hitler had felt himself pursued by calamity as one defensive line after another cracked. First came the Red Army's major offensive in Hungary, then the revolt by Tito's partisan bands in Yugoslavia, followed by the fall of the strongholds at Kolberg and Königsberg. Numerous less decisive items of alarming news reached him on a daily basis. In addition there were disagreements with his former chief of staff, Heinz Guderian, who had been relieved of his duties, and with Albert Speer, who, at the end of March, had stubbornly refused to express hope for "a successful continuation of the war." In response Hitler had said, "With treachery all around me, only misfortune has remained faithful to me—misfortune and my shepherd dog Blondi."

The one break in the series of reports bearing bad news seemed to come when Joseph Goebbels called the evening of April 13. His voice cracking with excitement, he shouted breathlessly into the phone, "My Führer, I congratulate you! It is written in the stars that the second half of April will be a turning point for us. Today is Friday, April thirteenth!" Then he informed Hitler that President Roosevelt had died. A meeting with generals, ministers, and party leaders was called immediately, and in response to astrological ascendancies, conjunctions of the planets, and crossings in the quadrant, long-extinguished hopes rose again. Holding a bunch of papers in his shaking hand, Hitler ran from person to person and, with an old man's manic excitability, held out the news reports, saying, "Here! You didn't want to believe it. Now tell me, who was right?" He reminded them of the House of Brandenburg and the miracle that saved Frederick the Great in 1762, when the death of the Czarina Elizabeth changed the course of the Seven Years War. Another miracle has occurred, he said. "The war is not lost! Here, read this! Roosevelt is dead."

As so often before in his life, Providence seemed to have seen reason and at the last minute come over to his side. Hitler had been trying for years to convince those around him that the "disgusting concubinage" of his enemies would soon break apart, and before the worst happened, England and the United States would recognize him as the champion of their common civilization opposing the barbarians from the East. Roosevelt's death, he now assured them, was the longed-for signal for a reversal of the alliances; the war in the West was as good as over. For a few hours a mood of exhilaration prevailed in the bunker, a feeling of confidence, of relief at having gotten away with it, and a renewed expectation of victory. But during the night, after these fantasies had run their course, depression set in again, especially when a report arrived that the Red Army had captured Vienna. According to one participant, Hitler sat in his armchair "exhausted and dazed but also relieved; even so, he seemed to have lost all hope." As it turned out, the death of the American president had no effect on the course of the war.

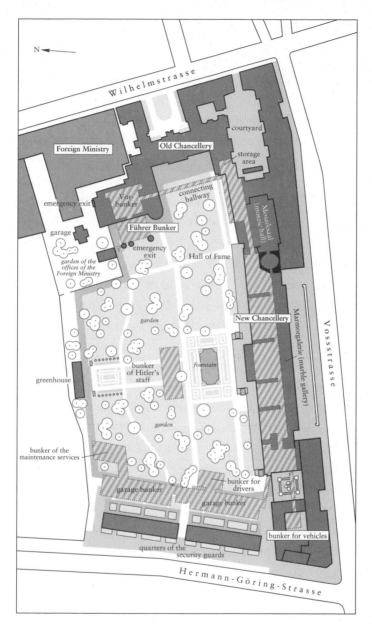

Layout of the extensive bunker system on the grounds of the Reich Chancellery

Hitler had returned to Berlin in January, after the failed Ardennes offensive. At first he moved into quarters in the New Reich Chancellery, but the relentless air raids soon drove him out and forced him into the deep underground bunker where, in the opinion of several observers, he felt he could finally be himself. The phobias he was subject to all his life had surfaced as early as 1933. Just a few months after he was appointed chancellor that year, he ordered a series of alterations to be made in the Reich Chancellery. One of his insistent demands was for the construction of a bunkerlike cellar under the building. Just how obsessive his desire was is revealed during his discussions with Albert Speer about architecture. He kept drawing "bunkers, again and again, bunkers." Even the banquet hall that the architect Leonhard Gall designed for him in 1935 in the garden behind the Chancellery had an underground air-raid shelter with a ceiling that was almost eight feet thick. This was later reinforced with an additional three feet of concrete. Then, three years later, during the construction of Speer's New Reich Chancellery, extensive additional shelters were built. In the lower levels of the building and stretching the full length of Voßstrasse there were now more than ninety concrete cells, connected to the bunker under the banquet hall by an underground corridor some 260 feet long.

In the winter of 1941, when the disastrous defeat of the German army before the gates of Moscow once again stirred up Hitler's anxiety, he considered even this sprawling bunker system insufficient. In 1942, although his armies occupied immense stretches of territory from Stalingrad to Hammerfest in northern Norway, and all the way south to Tripoli, he commissioned Speer's office to draw up plans for the construction of an additional catacomb that would be several feet deeper.

It connected with the shelter under the banquet hall, which was thereafter called the *Vorbunker* (ante-bunker), and contained a canteen for use by Hitler's closest associates, several lounges or common rooms and bedrooms, as well as a kitchen and servants' quarters—sixteen rooms altogether. Construction crews once again invaded the garden behind the Reich Chancellery, with its stand of old trees and quiet park paths. Only a few generations earlier, Bettina von Arnim had written to Goethe that she was living "here in a paradise." Now the work crews felled the trees and brought in construction supplies, cement mixers, reinforcement material, and piles of lumber. By early 1945 the concrete monstrosity that was to be the Führer Bunker was almost completed, but work on the shelters and guard towers continued for some time and wasn't even finished in April.

The bunkers under the New Reich Chancellery contained the living quarters of Hitler's entourage: his powerful secretary, Martin Bormann; his last army chief of staff, General Hans Krebs, and his aides; General Burgdorf; Hitler's chief pilot, General Hans Baur; SS Gruppenführer Hermann Fegelein, who served as Himmler's representative at the Führer's head-quarters; as well as countless officers, secretaries, guards, order-lies, radio operators, cartographers, and other personnel. Several of the rooms were furnished as an emergency sick bay; some were used as a place of refuge for bomb victims, pregnant women, and about two hundred children. Their numbers increased daily and soon led to unbearable overcrowding.

The *Vorbunker* was connected to the Führer Bunker by a circular staircase. The dimensions of the concrete ceiling have not been recorded. But since the floor, with its almost seven-foot-thick foundation slab, was about forty feet below the

Hitler and his all-powerful secretary, Martin Bormann, in 1943

garden level and there was a nearly nine-foot-high section in between that housed the life-support equipment and storage areas, the thickness of the ceiling was estimated to be almost thirteen feet. In a memorable characterization from the early 1930s, Konrad Heiden, the first Hitler biographer, characterized the Führer's real persona—that mixture of pathos, boastfulness, and aggressiveness—as "*Prahlereien auf der Flucht*," "boasting while on the run." Now, with Hitler retreating into the deep bunker and issuing victory slogans from there, this observation—once considered absurd by many—began to match reality.

The Führer Bunker consisted of about twenty small, sparsely furnished rooms. The one exception was the corridor or anteroom in front of Hitler's private apartment, which was furnished with an upholstered bench and a few old armchairs. Several paintings hung on the walls. Next to the anteroom was the conference room in which military or situation conferences took place—up to twenty people would crowd around a map table in a 150-square-foot space. These conferences went on for many hours, several times a day.

Hitler's two private rooms, a study and a bedroom, were also scantily furnished. A Dutch still life hung over the sofa in his study, and above his desk, in an oval frame, was a portrait of Frederick the Great by Anton Graff. Hitler would sit in front of it, brooding absentmindedly, as though he were in silent conversation with the king. At the foot of the bed stood a strongbox in which Hitler kept his personal papers. In one corner—as had been the case at his headquarters in Rastenburg—there was an oxygen tank to ease his constant worry that he would not be able to breathe if the diesel generators that provided the bunker with light, heat, and fresh air broke down.

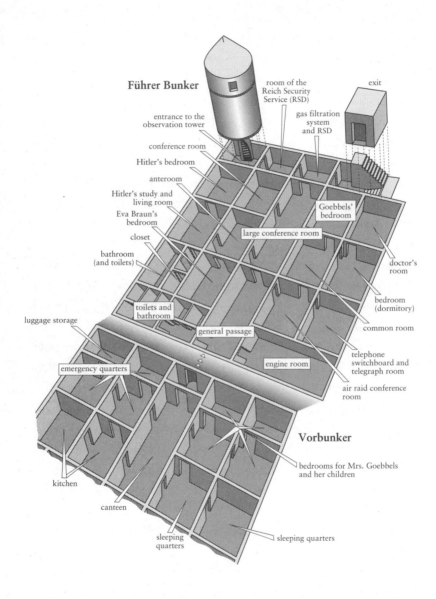

Führer Bunker

entrance to the observation tower

conference room

Hitler's bedroom

anteroom

Hitler's study and living room

Eva Braun's bedroom

closet

bathroom (and toilets)

room of the Reich Security Service (RSD)

gas filtration system and RSD

exit

Goebbels' bedroom

large conference room

doctor's room

bedroom (dormitory)

common room

luggage storage

toilets and bathroom

general passage

emergency quarters

engine room

telephone switchboard and telegraph room

air raid conference room

Vorbunker

bedrooms for Mrs. Goebbels and her children

kitchen

canteen

sleeping quarters

sleeping quarters

Layout of the *Vorbunker* or "ante-bunker" and the somewhat deeper Führer Bunker in the garden of the Reich Chancellery

In each of the rooms, naked lightbulbs hung from the ceiling, casting cold light on the faces of those who were there and adding to the impression that they were all moving about in a ghost world. In the final days, the water supply occasionally failed and an almost unbearable stench spread from the *Vorbunker*— exhaust fumes from the constantly humming diesel engines, mixed with the pungent smell of urine and human perspiration. Oily puddles collected in some of the corridors leading to the deep bunker, and for a time drinking water had to be rationed. Several witnesses have described the oppressive effect the cramped quarters, concrete, and artificial light had on people's spirits. In his diaries Goebbels wrote that he avoided these rooms as much as possible, so as not to fall prey to the "desolate mood." It's easy to understand how this remote netherworld setting contributed to the unreal decrees promulgated from there, decrees in which ghost divisions were assembled for offensive operations that never took place, and outflanking maneuvers were launched that existed only in Hitler's fantasy.

Hitler himself seems to have been most visibly ravaged by this hellish cave existence thirty-three feet below the surface. For years his skin had had a pasty look, but of late his facial features had become puffy, bloated. The heavy, dark pouches under his eyes became more and more noticeable. Markedly stooped, he walked with a peculiar gait, lurching from side to side, moving along close to the bunker walls as though looking for support. Some perceptive observers had the impression that he was accentuating his frailty for dramatic effect. For the first time Hitler also showed signs of slovenliness. His clothes, which had always been painfully correct, were splattered with food stains; cake crumbs stuck to the corners of his mouth, and whenever he held his eyeglasses in his left hand during a situation conference report, they would clatter softly against the tabletop. Then he would put the eyeglasses down, as though he had been caught. The trembling hand contradicted his view that anything could be achieved by willpower. "My hand may tremble," he assured a delegation of veterans, "but even if my head were to tremble, my heart never will."

"He knew the game was up," a general staff officer noted, "and he no longer had the strength to conceal it. He was in terrible physical shape, dragging himself along slowly and laboriously from his living quarters to the bunker conference room, throwing his upper body forward and pulling his legs along. His sense of balance was impaired; if he stopped to talk to someone on this short sixty-to-ninety-foot walk, he would have to sit down on one of the benches that had been placed for that purpose along both walls or hold on to whoever he was talking to. . . . His eyes were bloodshot, and even though all written material intended for him was typed in letters three times normal size on special 'Führer typewriters,' he could only make out the writing by using eyeglasses with strong lenses. Saliva often trickled from the corners of his mouth. . . ."

Some thought that Hitler was also deteriorating mentally with every passing day. After he returned from the nightly situation conferences, usually around six o'clock in the morning, he would sink down on his sofa to dictate instructions for the next day. One of the secretaries reported that as soon as she entered the room, he would get up with a great deal of effort, "and sit down again on the sofa, exhausted. His valet would then prop up his feet. He would lie there, completely apathetic, thinking only of . . . chocolate and cake. His craving for cake had become pathological. Before, he used to eat three pieces of cake at most, but now he had them fill his plate to overflowing three times." And another secretary complained about the monotony of his conversation: "In the last few weeks, [this man] who used to speak so passionately about all kinds of subjects, talked only about dogs and dog training, food and nutrition, and the stupidity and wickedness of the world."

Only in front of visitors did he manage to pull himself out of these depressions, recapturing his hypnotic power and persuasiveness. Frequently he would use a recollection, such as the name of an admired military leader or a fine-sounding triviality, to give himself and his visitor new encouragement. He would seize on casually dropped references, fantasizing them into powerfully growing armies that were already on their way to fight the war's decisive battle outside the gates of the capital. In any case, he intimated, the Russians used soldiers from conquered countries, "*Beutesoldaten*," to fight their battles, so their alleged superiority was "the biggest bluff since Genghis Khan." And again and again he would refer to "miracle weapons" that were going to bring about a turning point in the war and put all the fainthearted to shame.

In spite of his progressive infirmity, Hitler did not relinquish control of military operations. A firm belief in his mission combined with sheer willpower provided him with renewed bursts of energy. These were reinforced by a consuming distrust that made him suspect his generals of wanting to ridicule or expose him, perhaps even to get Dr. Morell, his personal physician, to drug him and then have him removed from Berlin. And although he usually had himself under control, he would on occasion fly into a rage. Once he faced his army chief of staff, General Heinz Guderian, snorting with anger, fists raised, his entire body trembling. Shortly thereafter, in late March, Guderian was dismissed.

Hitler became more isolated, more solitary. A few times one of the bunker inhabitants saw him laboriously making his way up the narrow staircase that led to the garden exit. But halfway up he turned back, exhausted, and, as he so often did, went to the washroom next to the middle corridor, where the dogs were kept. There, with a strangely vacant expression, he played for a long time with his shepherd bitch and her five puppies, which had been whelped in early April.

Aboveground, beyond the massive concrete walls, reigned the random chaos of a war now ending in exhaustion, misery, and fear of retaliation. None of the shrill, twisted slogans the government propaganda machine incessantly churned out matched this reality and its endless mortal terrors. True, for a minority the basic repertoire of catch phrases about faith, honor, and loyalty still had their effect. But most people had long since come to distrust these emotional appeals. Anyone who had his wits about him, or who had come to his senses in the face of the approaching end, had by now had enough of the "hold out to the last man" and "bulwark" slogans in which the German Reich was raised to the role of solitary hero battling the latest Horsemen of the Apocalypse, namely, world Jewry, Bolshevism, and plutocracy. Other slogans invoked the joy and honor of fighting for a lost cause and celebrated the idealized contempt for life that in the past had exercised such a dark power over German hearts and minds. With German battle lines disintegrating on all fronts, the lack of defense and weapons, and the never-ending horrors of daily life, it was im-

possible not to sense the hollowness of such public pronounce-
ments as "Revenge is our virtue! Hate is our duty! Bravely and
loyally, proudly and defiantly, will we turn our fortifications
into mass graves for the Soviet hordes. . . . We all know that
the hour before sunrise is always the darkest. Remember that
during the battle, when the blood runs into your eyes and
darkness is all about you. No matter what happens, victory will
be ours. Death to the Bolsheviks! Long live the Führer!"

Soon after the start of the major Soviet offensive, Hitler had
ordered all available forces to be sent east to defend Berlin
along the Oder River. Since then, hardly any experienced or
adequately equipped troops were left in and around the city itself. Berlin had been declared a "fortress" on February 1, and its
commandant, Lieutenant General Hellmuth Reymann, had
repeatedly stated that he needed at least 200,000 battle-tested
soldiers to defend it adequately. Instead he had less than half
that number, a motley bunch gathered from the remnants of a
tank corps, the guard regiment, a few random units from various branches of the service, as well as about forty *Volkssturm*
battalions composed mostly of old men and some four thousand teenage Hitler Youths. In addition, several engineer battalions and antiaircraft teams were deployed within the city
limits. The SS and police units assembled in Berlin were not
under Reymann's command, however. Hitler rejected all his requests for reinforcements, saying that sufficient troops, tanks,
and weapons were available if a battle for Berlin had to be
fought.

Even more serious was the lack of an agreed-upon plan for
the defense of the city. Operations that required tried and
tested collaboration had to be improvised hastily for each situation. On top of that, Reymann found himself entangled in

Call-up of the last reserves: a fifteen-year-old and an older soldier who were supposed to stem the attack of the far superior Soviet elite units on the streets of Berlin

constant squabbles over authority. Sometimes instructions came from the Wehrmacht High Command headed by Field Marshal Wilhelm Keitel, another time from Army Chief of Staff Krebs, and occasionally from General Heinrici. And Hitler constantly broke into the chain of command with erratic ideas, so that Reymann never knew clearly just where he stood.

The organizational chaos was compounded by Goebbels, who, in addition to being Berlin Gauleiter (Party district leader) was also the Commissioner of Reich Defense. An advocate of "total war," Goebbels had been unable to fulfill his vision because it had met with resistance from all sides; now he saw an opportunity to implement his plan after all. He had just obtained Hitler's permission to set up battalions composed of women. In the discussions about the construction of field fortifications and deployment of troops he now jealously insisted that he alone was responsible for the defense of the city. Characteristically, he also considered Reymann to be under his command, and deemed it important that the commandant come to *his* office for all discussions. The lack of clarity over responsibilities, constant staff changes, and confusion as to the chain of command, as well as the contradictory information about available troops and resources, resulted in a hopeless muddle that did more to hinder the defense of the city than to further it.

In addition, Goebbels put out his own "Defense Orders," paying no attention to the commands issued by the military. Every Monday he called a "Major War Council" attended by all the commanders, the senior SS and SA leaders, the *Oberbürgermeister* (mayor of the city), and Berlin's chief of police, as well as the most influential representatives of industry. He also sent out his *Greiftrupps* on a daily basis, squads assigned to comb through business firms and city agencies for people fit for service at the front. But the number of eligible bodies he was able to muster was negligible and impressed no one, even though he managed to transform the small groups of dejected civilians he was able to round up into regiments of impatient fighters itching to be sent into battle "for Führer and Fatherland."

Everything else was in short supply, too: tanks, artillery, rifles, fuel, and trench-digging tools of every sort. In the Tiergarten, *Volkssturm* units practiced maneuvers against the enemy by crawling across the grounds while their comrades, hiding in the bushes, beat sticks on empty tin cans to simulate machine-gun fire. Elsewhere they used rolls of cardboard to train in the use of bazookas (*Panzerfaust*) and constructed roadblocks with cobblestones, bedframes, trucks demolished in air raids, and all sorts of junk. Each *Volkssturm* member was supplied with five rounds of ammunition—provided he had even been given a weapon—only to face another predicament. While the weapons were mostly of German or Czech manufacture, the ammunition came from Italy, France, and other countries that had fought with or against Germany. In addition to the hunting and sporting guns that citizens had had to turn in, there were more than fifteen different types of firearms and countless varieties of ammunition. Nothing matched, a reflection of the disorganization that was spreading throughout Germany.

Units of the *Volkssturm* or the Wehrmacht would march down a major thoroughfare to the defense of one of the suburbs while, on the other side of the same road, units were approaching from the opposite direction, assigned to protect Tempelhof Airport or Westhafen, the western port near the inner city. General Reymann declared that anyone not fit to bear arms could leave the city. At the same time Goebbels had a notice posted on the front door of every house, according to which "on orders from the Führer . . . all men between the ages of 15 and 70" had to report for military service, no exceptions. "Any coward who slips away into the air-raid shelters," the posters concluded, "will be court-martialed and put to death."

Only the propaganda experts seemed undaunted. Day after day they trotted out the "best horse in their stable" as Goebbels cynically put it, before the frightened populace, describing in great detail the horror of the "bolshevization of Europe": great mounds of slaughtered citizens, raped women, and butchered children. As Bormann remarked, this "same old stuff," could be "continually replayed with variations," like player-piano rolls, and the horrific images would instill in people an immense determination to fight, perhaps even causing the enemy coalition to break apart.

Since the Berlin newspapers had ceased publication in mid-April, carefully planted rumors were used as an alternative means for raising the morale of the populace. According to "reliable sources," allied successes were nothing more than a ruse by the Führer, who had intentionally lured the enemy deep into the country so as to destroy him more effectively and completely. Or, it was whispered, General Krebs had contacted the Russians and reminded the Soviet dictator that he, Krebs, had been the German military attaché in Moscow. Stalin had publicly embraced him and even kissed him, supposedly deeply "moved," and had conjured up the spirit of their former "brotherhood in arms." Then the opinion of an "expert army officer" made the rounds: The bombing campaign, which had gone on for years and which had been endured with helpless despair, was really a lucky break because it had prepared Berlin for hand-to-hand fighting in this decisive hour. And, as military history has shown, the defender's position in house-to-house fighting is without exception always superior to that of the attacker. There was also talk about submarines carrying "stratospheric missiles" that would destroy New York, and "ice grenades" spewing caustic smoke that would corrode everything. The populace treated these bizarre rumors with growing, often biting, skepticism. Propaganda, went one common saying, was like the orchestra on board a sinking ship, whose members continued to play cheery tunes even as they were being sucked into the ocean depths—because the shipping company's management controlled all the sheet music.

More indicative of the actual situation and the prevailing mood were the motorized general courts-martial that were constantly looking for deserters, charging through the streets, searching through homes, businesses, and rubble fields. At the slightest suspicion they shot or hanged "traitors" on the spot. On February 15, 1945, Hitler ordered special courts responsible for all crimes "that threaten German fighting strength or determination to fight" to be established. These courts consisted of a criminal judge and a Party representative, as well as an officer from the Wehrmacht or the Waffen SS. Ten days later Himmler set up a corps of "Special Drumhead Courts-Martial," and on March 9 a "Flying Drumhead Court-Martial" was established under Lieutenant General Rudolf Hübner, who received instructions directly from Hitler. It seemed as though only threats of punishment could maintain even a modicum of confidence.

Informants told the security service (SD) in mid-April that faith in the leadership was slipping away "like an avalanche" among broad circles of the population. An angry Goebbels had to admit that more and more government officials were simply disappearing, "vanishing into thin air"; the Party was "pretty much finished." In some districts of Berlin, residents were outraged to see the bodies of dozens of people who had been executed since mid-March hanging from trees and lampposts and, as an even stronger deterrent, on street barricades and tank obstacles. Understandably, no reliable data exist, but judicious estimates maintain that close to a thousand were executed in the last three months of the regime. Some military leaders, like Major General Hans Mummert, commander of the Müncheberg tank division, were so upset by these wild goings-on that they instructed their troops to approach the special courts-martial with drawn weapons, if necessary.

It was easy to see that defeat was inescapable. Anything that came after would be a war beyond the end of the war. And yet, far on the distant horizon, some foolish hopes still flickered. Gerda Bormann, Martin Bormann's wife, wrote to her husband that the situation reminded her of the Götterdämmerung in the *Edda*. "The Giants and the Dwarfs, the wolf Fenris and the snake Mitgard, all the powers of evil . . . are storming over the bridge of the gods. . . . The citadel of the gods is tottering and all seems lost. But suddenly a new citadel rises, more beautiful than the one before, and Baldur lives again." She was taking a familiar escape route, away from reality into the platitudes of myth. But even that route soon came to an end. It did not lead past ruined landscapes of burned-out cities, streams of refugees crowding the roads and growing chaos everywhere, with the Allies inexorably conquering ever-larger regions of the country in the east as well as the west. German resistance was visibly broken. In some remote places, tired, disintegrating units fought on, but no command from the Führer could reach them anymore. Hitler, meanwhile, controlled only a few fanatically devoted outposts and a rapidly shrinking area around the capital.

And yet, in those last days of the war there seemed to be a desperate energy at work, set on turning defeat into catastrophe. If we don't win, Hitler had said in the early thirties in one of his reveries about the impending war, "then even as we go down we will take half the world down with us." Now he was about to make his prediction come true.

TWO

Hitler in German History:
Consistency or Catastrophe?

Was the end foreseeable? The question has not yet been put to rest. Were the devastated, barren landscape and the concrete cubes of the Führer Bunker already discernible behind the charming Old Prussian façade of the historical palace that was the Reich Chancellery on Wilhelmstrasse? Was Hitler the all but inevitable consequence of the country's history? Was he a product of German consistency rather than, to quote the historian Friedrich Meinecke, a German catastrophe?

The shock wave of rapturous enthusiasm that followed Hitler's seizure of power, even though it was created and relentlessly escalated by clever theatrical staging, would at first glance refute all claims that it was a historical accident. True, even in the midst of all the jubilation, torchlight parades, mass rallies, demonstrations, and nightly mountaintop bonfires that were part of the spring of 1933, there were palpable feelings of uncertainty, and for quite some time people were still asking themselves whether the country was not letting itself in for a crazy or, at any rate, a somewhat eerie adventure under the new rulers. But the headlong violence with which the National Socialists forced their way into key political positions had its own baffling power of persuasion. It soon seemed to many that the Weimar Republic had been nothing more than a brief interlude, and so there was no lasting memory, no touch of reverence, to make the leave-taking difficult. After many years of statehood gone awry, the determination to try again emerged, as if on cue, sweeping away all misgivings among a fast-growing majority of the people. At the same time, the "New Order" that instantly took shape not only gained supporters and justification despite its inferior banality, but, as its ringleaders incessantly crowed, the future belonged to them.

It was these circumstances accompanying the seizure of power which gave future historians the impression that after years of being forced to adapt to democracy, a constitutional state, and "Western" values, the Germans had reverted to their true selves and to the former repulsive role they had supposedly played in European history. The first contemporary interpretations of these events often constructed long genealogies—from Arminius, the Teutonic chief of the Cherusci (who defended German lands against the Romans in A.D. 9), and the medieval emperors, right up to Frederick the Great and Bismarck. At every turn a latent Hitlerism was discovered that had existed long before the advent of Hitler. Thus, no matter how one looked at things, there were no "innocent" events or individuals in German history. The specters of subservience and narrowness even lurked in the idyllic bourgeois period that preceded the revolution of March 1848, and anyone with any insight could see that Germany had a special secret mission, a calling *in* the world and, if need be, *against* it, too. According to this view, German Romanticism was nothing but a tendency toward cruelty and hatred of the world, concealed behind deceptively tender images, a longing to return "to the forests" that had always been more familiar to this peculiar people than civilization, constitutionality, and human rights. SS leader Reinhard Heydrich, who was instrumental in organizing the Final Solution and who chaired the infamous Wannsee Conference, became for a time the incarnation of this kind of token stereotype of a German. He played the violin and could be deeply stirred by a Schubert sonata.

On the whole, such rather superficial portrayals of the character and history of Germany have been largely discredited, since they rationalized the National Socialist belief that Hitler was not only the legitimate heir of Prussia and Bismarck Germany, but also the man destined to fulfill German history. However, the much-debated question of which threads lead from Germany's past to Hitler and the ideological premises that made possible or even abetted his rise to power remains unanswered.

To make sense of it, historians have traced various trends back into the distant past. There was the German aversion to reality and arrogant concept of culture, one that despised politics or in any case did not know what to make of it. Then there were the conservative elements in the social fabric, the leanings toward authoritarian state structures, as well as the frequently and grimly emphasized reactionary nature of the power elite, whose preeminence had remained unchallenged because the German middle class had never developed a civic consciousness. These and some other characteristics supposedly led to a tradition of social discipline that had existed all along, in a kind of pre-totalitarian state of readiness. Add to that the customary weakness of the country's political institutions, and the German people's susceptibility to a charismatic leader becomes understandable, the prerequisite being, of course, that his decrees feed into the particular German mentality: the prevailing mood with its sense of deprivation and its encirclement complexes on the one hand, and, on the other, the tendency to turn everyday affairs into life-and-death decisions and to mythologize all politics.

Many of these considerations, some of which have become the subject of countless arguments, especially the one about the so-called "special path" followed by the Germans, can doubtlessly be connected with the emergence of Hitler. But history is a far more open field than it may seem to the historian looking for clues to the origins of a phenomenon after it has occurred; his insights are necessarily determined by questions he would never have asked had he not known the outcome. One must also take into account that similar events, of quite different consequence, can be found in the history of nearly every nation, at least on the European continent. In the case of Germany, a direct connection with Hitler can't easily be drawn without indulging in a good deal of speculation. It should also be said that any forces resisting his rise to power were crippled by the unique course of the nation's history. Nor is there an easy answer to a related question: Why did National Socialism show so much more ruthlessness and inhumanity than most other extremist movements of the twenties and thirties?

On closer examination, and adhering to the more plausible interpretations, the cold dose of reality following Germany's defeat in the fall of 1918 must be reckoned as a special German circumstance. Until the armistice, the country had been dreaming the 1870–71 dream of becoming a great power and of the "glorious times" ahead. Then suddenly it was confronted by an upheaval in its familiar way of life—a revolution that the vast majority of Germans saw only as "an uprising of the rabble"—which threw into disorder all the standards that had prevailed for so long. There was chaos in the streets, prolonged hunger, massive unemployment on an unprecedented scale, and social unrest that swept through entire provinces. Then came the Treaty of Versailles, presented to the public with pompous talk of peace but actually dictated by hypocrisy, vindictiveness, and spiteful shortsightedness. Its Article 231, referred to by Germans as the "war guilt clause," was intended by the victors and interpreted by the vanquished as a humiliation. It was Germany's expulsion from the circle of respected nations that disturbed its people more than any of the material burdens the victors placed on the country. One observer remarked that a "community of embittered people" had already sprung up, waiting only for a leader, someone to give them a signal. Inflation that brought with it the impoverishment of large sections of the population and the worldwide economic crisis that erupted a few years later intensified popular anger. Germans blamed the Weimar Republic, which was now beset from all sides, for these and innumerable other debacles raining down on them.

As the thirties began, Hitler exploited these emotions and the people's growing anger, deploring the crisis in speeches he delivered from one end of the country to the other, at the same time escalating the situation with every means at his disposal. It was his most promising path to power. Hitler's rapid rise has been explored endlessly, and so far has never been explained satisfactorily. No explanation is complete, however, without acknowledging that Hitler rose to the top in a spiritually broken nation. At the same time, the rush to embrace him and his movement was, more than anything else, a mindless escape from the luckless Weimar Republic. As one of its despairing defenders called it, the "state with the dunce cap" was pushed around and derided by far too many on the outside while those on the inside were united only in their contempt and hatred of the status quo.

This obscured an understanding of the deep moral fracture that many critics today perceive as having existed in 1933 in light of the later atrocities committed by the regime. Observers at the time either did not recognize it at all or only saw glimpses. Hardly anyone alive at the time had the remotest idea of the nature of the emerging totalitarian dictatorship and the degree of disenfranchisement, despotism, and violence it would bring to a country that ranked as one of the world's leading civilized nations. Even those who opposed the new rulers could not have imagined how far things would go. The great majority expected to see an authoritarian regime like Mussolini's in Italy, where, as everyone knew, the trains were running on time again. After the Weimar confusion, people yearned for the return of the many German "punctualities" they had missed for fourteen unbearably long years.

Among the peculiarly German circumstances, the one essential element that cannot be overestimated was Hitler himself. All the deductions laboriously drawn from history and the body politic, no matter how comprehensive or insightful, must in the final analysis return to Hitler and his personal history, which decisively put in motion the events that followed. None of the other countries affected by similar upheavals during the period between the wars had a leader who could match Hitler in oratorical power, organizational ability, tactical genius, and radicalness.

When it came to power politics, Hitler could also build on some relatively recent legacies, such as the idea that eastern Europe was the natural so-called *Lebensraum* or "living space" for the German Reich. Discussions of Germany's goals during World War I had in fact included "ethnic reallocation" and resettlement of extensive areas. The concept of an "ideal" alliance, which meant forging the closest possible ties with the British Empire, was something Hitler had been thinking about, at least in outline form, for some time. Such an alliance between the German people and their Germanic "cousins" on the other side of the Channel would make them the "controlling powers of the world."

The most urgent task in German politics, however, was to free the country of the dictates of the Treaty of Versailles. Here was Hitler's opportunity to win over the old ruling classes, still grieving over their failed ambition to turn Germany into a great power. A 1926 memorandum from the Reichswehr (the German Army, 1921–35) to the Foreign Office outlined a set of medium-term guidelines for German foreign policy: first, liberation of the Rhineland and the Saar; then the elimination of the Polish Corridor between the Reich and East Prussia; the return of Polish Upper Silesia; the annexation of Austria; and, finally, the occupation of the demilitarized zone. Except for the actual sequence of events, this was Hitler's foreign policy program during the 1930s. In spite of all their misgivings about his all-or-nothing moods and his brigand's personality, the old elite saw the leader of the Nazi Party as the man who could implement their revisionist intentions. He knew, like no one else, how to mobilize the nation, crossing all barriers by exploiting the widespread feeling of national humiliation growing out of the Versailles Treaty.

What his supporters and accomplices did not take into consideration, and presumably had no inkling of, was Hitler's determination to take his visions—a strange mixture of fantasy and ice-cold calculation—literally. They assumed incorrectly that his tirades about war, a New World Order, and a huge empire extending to the Urals and beyond had their origin in the momentary inspirations of a runaway temperament. Whereas they wanted to overcome the "humiliation" inflicted on them by the victors and restore the old borders, even adding some territory, Hitler's political program called for neither old nor new borders. What he wanted was to acquire new "living space"—millions of square miles of conquered land, as he remarked on one occasion, depopulated of those engaged in "the devil's work." Behind this lay an insatiable hunger for more land, with each acquisition being regarded merely as a launching pad for further advances.

There are those who believe that even these ideas did not break historical continuity, that basically they had already been espoused by the Pan-Germans and in Erich Ludendorff's 1918 plans for the East. Where the two lines of thought diverged was in the ideological ferment with which Hitler's were charged— his wild ideas about a global sickness, racial poisoning, the elimination of "weak elements," and renewal of the bloodline to "save the planet Earth." He had added a new theme that went beyond the naïve, imperialistic greed that informed his earlier thinking—a racial utopia that promised to lead to a new age. It was to be won and sustained by several hundred million genetically conscious people resolutely following their historic mission, conquering land and exterminating all "inferior races," or holding them in subjugation. There would be a "New Man" who razed everything to the ground, resettled territories, and sought relaxation from his historic mission by engaging in joyful "community folklore" in huge KdF (*Kraft durch Freude,* or Strength Through Joy) hotels on the Channel Islands, the Norwegian fjords, or in the Crimea. It was a break with everything the world had ever stood for. Trying to invent an origin for this revolution—an origin it did not have—is to fall retrospectively for the regime's own propaganda. The origins of this monstrous program were entirely self-generated. No one had ever gone to such extremes, and with such utter madness. It cannot therefore be argued that Hitler's vision is the culmination of a historic trend going back to Bismarck, Frederick the Great, or even to the medieval emperors.

What differentiated Hitler from any conceivable predecessors was the complete lack of a sense of responsibility beyond the merely personal, of any clear-headed, selfless ethos of service, and of any historic morality. In a letter to Hitler dated March 28, 1945, Albert Speer rebuked him for equating the existence of Germany with his own life span, describing this as an egocentricity unparalleled in history. Toward the end— more so than in the early, daredevil days that started with the occupation of the Rhineland in 1936, when he trembled for twenty-four hours awaiting his fate, until the occupation of Prague in the spring of 1939—Hitler revealed that he was only a gambler turned politician, who had gambled everything, and lost. Beyond that yawned nothingness.

On one of the last days in the bunker, Hitler's chief military adjutant, Wilhelm Burgdorf, a radical Party general who prided

Hitler's chief adjutant, General Wilhelm Burgdorf. At the end of April 1945, during a heated argument with Martin Bormann, Burgdorf pointed out that he had drawn the contempt of his fellow officers upon himself because of his total devotion to their common goal.

himself on his "limitless devotion" to *Führer und Volk,* clashed with Hitler's all-powerful secretary, Martin Bormann. In the course of their noisy argument, Burgdorf shouted that his unconditional devotion to the common cause had drawn the contempt of his fellow officers, who had accused him of being a "traitor." Now he was forced to admit that his opponents had been right, that his "idealism" had been "wrong," and that he himself had been "naïve and stupid." When General Krebs, a Hitler loyalist who witnessed the outburst, tried to intervene, Burgdorf fended him off: "Leave me alone, Hans; somebody has to say all this! Young officers went to their deaths by the hundreds of thousands." And for what, he was asking himself. The answer was, neither for the Fatherland nor for the future. Only now did he realize that "they died for *you*. . . . Millions of innocent human beings [were] sacrificed, while you, the leaders of the Party, enriched yourselves with the wealth of the people. You lived it up, amassed immense riches, stole *Junker* estates, built palaces, indulged in luxury, deceived and oppressed the people. You trampled our ideals into the mud, our morals, our belief, our soul. For you a human being was only a tool for your unquenchable hunger for power. You destroyed our centuries-old culture and the German people. This is your terrible burden of guilt."

There was complete silence in the bunker. Then Bormann, "cool, deliberate, and unctuous," said, "But, my dear man, there's no need to get personal. Even if others have all gotten rich, *I'm* free of guilt . . . *Prost!* [Cheers!]"

Before Burgdorf committed suicide a few days later, he would be proven right. After one of the last situation conferences on April 27, 1945, Hitler alluded to a remark by Richelieu and spoke about all the things he would have to forgo with his death—his big plans and "fondest memories." But then the gambler he had been all his life came to the fore again, the failed risk-taker, the man from nowhere who was about to disappear into the void, leaving behind him an endless trail of rubble and ruin. "What does it all mean?" he said with a dismissive gesture to the officers who were gathered around him. "At some point you have to leave all this rubbish behind anyway!"

THREE

"The War Is Lost!"

Hitler's fifty-sixth birthday, on April 20, brought the leaders of the regime together for the last time: Goebbels, Himmler, Bormann, Speer, Ley, Ribbentrop, and several Gauleiter (district party leaders), as well as the heads of the Wehrmacht. Göring had come from Karinhall, his hunting lodge. Early that morning he had dispatched to South Germany twenty-four trucks loaded with antiques, paintings, and furniture he had collected over the years. He would follow later. As soon as the column of vehicles was out of sight, he walked down his driveway toward the street. On the way there, his face showing no emotion, rather an almost businesslike calm, he inspected the preparations that had been made to blow up Karinhall. Glancing at the tangle of fuses, he said to the bodyguard at his side, "When you're Crown Prince, you have to do these things sometimes." Then he left for the birthday party. Eva Braun had arrived unexpectedly at the bunker a few days before, and had moved into the back rooms of the Führer's quarters.

The celebration was moved from the bunker to the larger, more festive rooms of the New Reich Chancellery. With paintings and furniture gone, and signs of repeated bomb damage, these quarters now seemed drab. Still, the gathering of so many uniformed dignitaries did bring back memories of the pomp and splendor so long dispensed with—even though the incessantly howling air-raid sirens further depressed the already bleak mood. After a few brief remarks, Hitler went from group to group, gravely, almost defensively, imploring, accepting congratulations, and offering words of encouragement. Although at first he seemed thoroughly exhausted and, as one of those present thought, had to work harder than usual to conceal the tremor in his left arm, the forced confidence he was communicating to others appeared to enliven him. To observers he seemed "galvanized." Meanwhile, outside on Wilhelmstrasse, the *Leibstandarte* (Hitler's personal SS division) marched in review past SS Gruppenführer Wilhelm Mohnke.

At some point that morning the codeword "Clausewitz" was issued, ordering a state of emergency. It also became known that, days before, Hitler had prepared for the eventuality of advancing enemy forces dividing the area. His plan was that the territory still remaining in German hands would be split into a Northern Command Zone, under Fleet Admiral Karl Dönitz, and a Southern Command Zone, under Field Marshal Albert Kesselring. For the well-wishers at the birthday party this desperate step was just another opportunity to praise the "military genius" of their Führer, who repeatedly managed to turn defensive situations into far more advantageous offensive positions. Goebbels described the two "command zones" as the arms of a "strategic pincer" that would prepare a "second Waterloo" for the unsuspecting Allies.

But in spite of all the deluded talk about tactical "strokes of genius" and an imminent victory—improbable though that might seem—most of those gathered there were anxious for the affair to end. All knew that the Red Army was about to complete its encirclement of the city and that there were only two constantly shrinking escape corridors left, one to the north and one to the south. At one point Göring sent an orderly to obtain a realistic estimate of how much longer they could still get through.

Hitler appeared to be dragging out the reception as though he sensed the disdain and impatience of most of those present and wanted to prevent them from leaving. Later, in the large conference room while discussing the strategic military situation, he ordered that the Soviet units, which had advanced to the outer defensive circle in the north and east, be pushed back with all possible force. Once again he was deploying troops that marched solely through his mad imagination and getting bogged down in tactical details, such as where to deploy a self-propelled antitank gun, or the best placement for a machine gun. The military officers listened to his instructions in silence, their expressions immobile. Only Göring—huge and massive—was having trouble hiding his restlessness as he sat opposite Hitler, seemingly counting the minutes that were elapsing in futile talk.

The previous evening Hitler had brought up the question of whether it wouldn't be more practical to give up the largely indefensible capital where, by now, there were hardly any German troops left. At the same time he indicated it was his intention to take charge in the Southern Command Zone and to

continue the fight from Obersalzberg, within sight of the leg-
endary Untersberg. Perhaps in an allusion to his own afterlife,
he once again mentioned the Emperor Barbarossa who, as tradition would have it, slept the "sleep of centuries" within the
mountain.

But Goebbels had passionately urged him to remain in
Berlin, and if death indeed was to be his fate, then to die in the
ruins of the city; he owed nothing less to his historical mission,
to the oaths he had once sworn, and to his place in history. The
Führer, Goebbels insisted, must not end his life in a "summer
house." There is reason to believe that this particular argument
influenced Hitler, who always saw his life unfolding on a grand
stage. Only in Berlin, Goebbels told him, could a "moral success on a global scale" be achieved.

Hitler now assured his listeners that he had sorted things
out during the night; he would remain in the capital. There
was a brief, stunned silence; then almost all in the large conference room implored him to leave Berlin, pointing out that the
last escape route might be closed off within a few hours. But
Hitler remained adamant. "How can I motivate the troops to
wage a decisive battle for Berlin if I escape to a safe place," he
insisted. Finally, to stop the arguing, he said he would leave this
decision to "fate"; but he would not prevent anyone else from
getting out. To show that his mind was made up, he counter-
manded the decisions of Heinrici and Busse, the commanders
in charge, and ordered the Fifty-sixth Tank Corps, led by
General Weidling, back to Berlin. The Fifty-sixth had been
involved in heavy defensive action ever since the battle over
the Seelow Heights.

Immediately after Hitler adjourned the conference, a pale
and perspiring Göring bade him good-bye, citing "urgent tasks

in South Germany." Hitler stared silently past him, as though he had long known about the shameful scheming of his deputy. He then went out into the garden behind the chancellery, accompanied by Goebbels, Himmler, Speer, and Bormann.

Some well-wishers had arrived late, and were waiting not far from the entrance near an area sown with bomb craters, tree stumps, and fallen trees: a delegation of battle-weary men from the Frundsberg SS Division and the Kurland army, as well as a number of Hitler Youths from a "Tank Destruction Unit." Hitler, hunched over as though hiding in his overcoat, walked up and down the rows of soldiers and shook hands with each of them. Then he went over to the Hitler Youths, patted some of them encouragingly, and handed out decorations. Mustering all his strength, he finally managed to utter a few sentences to the effect that the battle for Berlin must be won at all costs. In concluding, he called out in a tired voice, "*Heil euch!*" But no one answered. "All you could hear," Reich Youth Leader Artur Axmann noted in his report, "was the distant rumbling from the front, now scarcely nineteen miles away."

Once Hitler had returned to the bunker, the big exodus began. A long line of cabinet ministers and party chiefs pressed toward him; each said a few embarrassed or forced words of farewell, and left. They were followed by endless columns of trucks. One of Hitler's adjutants reported that Hitler, "profoundly disappointed, indeed shattered, merely nodded" and, "without saying a word," allowed these men "whom he had once made powerful" to leave.

While some took to their heels, others set out for the front accompanied by, as someone put it, the "fervent good wishes" of the people. At about 10 p.m. Hitler told those closest to him that he intended to "shake up" his staff. He sent two of his secretaries, several assistants, the stenographers, as well as his personal physician, Dr. Morell, to southern Germany. Perhaps he would follow later, he said as they were leaving. And to Morell he said, "Drugs can't help me anymore." Then, earlier than usual, he retired to his rooms. Some of those who had stayed joined Eva Braun and Martin Bormann for a small post-celebration party in the half-empty Führer apartment in the New Reich Chancellery. They ordered drinks to be brought in and tried to forget the eerie world of the bunker, dancing to music provided by the only phonograph record they could find. It was a song that spoke of "blood-red roses" and future happiness. Eventually, nearby artillery strikes drove them back into the bunker.

No sooner had the word spread that government leaders were free to leave, than applicants besieged the commandant's house near the Berlin Schloss for the required permits. More than two thousand travel documents were issued in the course of a few hours, even though Goebbels had ordered that no one capable of bearing arms be permitted to leave the city. That morning Otto Meissner, head of the Presidential Chancellery, had already checked in by telephone, reporting that he had gone to Mecklenburg in order to continue to perform his official duties there. Goebbels replied he was sorry that now he couldn't do what he had wanted to do for twelve long years— spit in Meissner's face. The evening before, in a congratulatory speech broadcast on the occasion of Hitler's birthday, Goebbels had said:

"Germany is still a land of loyalty. In the midst of danger this loyalty shall celebrate its greatest triumph. History will never be able to say that the people abandoned their Führer, or that the Führer abandoned his people. That is our victory! As [God] has so often done before when Lucifer stood before the

On his fifty-sixth birthday, on April 20, 1945, Hitler greeted a group of Hitler Youths who had seen action in Berlin. He decorated some of them. After a brief speech, and with the rumbling of artillery shelling in the background, he saluted them in a tired voice with *"Heil euch!"* There was no reply.

gates leading to power over all nations, He will hurl him down again into the abyss from which he came." The underworld will not rule this part of the earth, he continued, "rather, order, peace, and prosperity" will prevail. The Führer alone is "the core and center of resistance against the disintegration of the world." And two days later, in his last editorial for the weekly newspaper *Das Reich,* Goebbels demanded, with rousing vehemence, "resistance at any cost," even "by boys and girls who will hurl hand grenades and antitank mines down upon" the Asiatic attackers and "who will shoot out of windows and cellar openings, disregarding all danger."

The following morning Hitler was awakened at about nine-thirty, nearly two hours earlier than usual. He was informed that Russian artillery was firing into the center of the city. A little later the news came that the Brandenburg Gate, the Reichstag, and even the Friedrichsstrasse station had been hit by shells in quick succession. Shortly thereafter, Hitler, unshaven and visibly distraught, came into the anteroom. His first question was "What's going on? Where is all this shooting coming from?" When Burgdorf explained that the center of the city had apparently come under fire from an enemy position northeast of Zossen, Hitler turned pale. "Are the Russians that close already?" Then he asked to be connected with General Karl Koller, the Luftwaffe chief of staff. According to Koller's notes:

> Hitler called early in the morning.—"Do you know that Berlin is under artillery fire? The center of the city."—
> "No!"—"Don't you hear it?"—"No! I'm in the Werder Game Park." Hitler: "There's great concern in the city about long-range artillery bombardment. They say it's coming from a large-caliber railroad battery. The Russians are said to have

captured a railway bridge over the Oder. The Luftwaffe must spot this battery immediately and destroy it."—I: "The enemy has no railway bridge over the Oder. Maybe they were able to take one of our heavy batteries and swing it around. But it's probably the Russian field army's midsize guns; with these the enemy can now hit the center of the city." Long debate about railroad bridge over the Oder, whether or not the artillery of the Russian army can reach the center of Berlin. . . . Hitler insists that we must immediately spot the battery and attack it. He wants to know within ten minutes just where the battery is located. . . .

Koller's notes continue: "I call the division command post of the antiaircraft unit at the Zoo bunker. In answer to my question I am told that all this to-do is just about a 10-cm to 12-cm caliber gun. The antiaircraft unit observed the Russian battery taking up its position in Marzahn that morning; distance to the center of the city, about seven and a half miles. . . . Hitler greets my report on the facts of the situation with disbelief."

Koller's notes on this telephone conversation illustrate Hitler's delusional mood and his characteristic bias in dealing with generals as well as with reality. Without knowing the details, he speaks of "long-range shelling" and freely invents railway batteries and bridges over the Oder. But more than merely revealing that he had insufficient or even distorted information, his words underscore the confusion that existed within the leadership at headquarters. Koller's April 21 notes continue:

A short while later, Hitler again on the telephone. He wants exact figures regarding the ongoing deployment of aircraft south of Berlin. I reply that such information can no longer be immediately provided because the lines of communication with the troops are not functioning reliably. One has to be content, I tell him, with the regular morning and evening reports that come in routinely. That infuriates him.

Shortly thereafter Hitler telephoned again, and again. He wanted information about jet planes stationed near Prague; then he asked about the "private army" Göring was allegedly maintaining; and he referred to a letter from the industrialist Hermann Röchling. Suddenly he screamed, "All the leaders of the Luftwaffe ought to be strung up at once!" And on and on like that, nonstop: questions, orders, retractions, with short operational lectures in between. "Who the hell knows what that was all about?" a confused General Koller wrote. One can almost hear him sigh with frustration.

To get an overview of the situation, Koller decided to get in touch with General Krebs. After many futile attempts, he finally reached Krebs at 10:30 p.m. and tried to obtain some clarification about a diversionary attack by SS General Steiner, mentioned by Hitler but about which he himself knew nothing. Hitler unexpectedly cut in. "Suddenly," notes Koller, "I hear his agitated voice on the line: 'Do you still have doubts about my order? I think I expressed myself clearly enough. All Luftwaffe forces in the Northern Zone that can be made available for ground action must immediately be supplied to Steiner. Anyone who holds back any units will forfeit his life within five hours. Your own head is on the line.'"

A little later Hitler became indignant when none of the stenographers—whom he himself dismissed only hours before—showed up in the conference room where an officer was presenting the situation report. As always, he had only one word to

explain any disillusioning setback: "Betrayal!" Later that night
Walter Hewel, the Foreign Ministry's permanent representative
on the Führer's staff, whom Hitler held in high esteem, asked
for last-minute instructions and reminded him that this was
the very last chance for political action. Hitler got up. "As he
slowly and wearily leaves the room, his feet dragging, he says in
a soft, completely changed voice: 'Politics? I don't get involved
in politics anymore. I detest politics. When I'm dead, you'll have
plenty of political decisions to make.'"

Nerves were frazzled, and more and more frequently the
dam, forged of intransigence and false confidence in victory,
burst. During Goebbels's last press conference, held by candlelight in his residence behind windows nailed over with cardboard, the propaganda minister heaped all blame for the failure
of the Great Plan on the officer corps and the "reactionaries"
with whom they had been compelled to ally themselves. Repeatedly and at great length, he went on about how the old
caste had always betrayed him, how rearmament had been neglected in peacetime, how wrong decisions were made during
the campaigns against France and the Soviet Union, and how
Germany—from the start of the Allied invasion right up to
July 20—had failed to act.

When an official in the Propaganda Ministry, Assistant Secretary Hans Fritzsche, interjected that one should remember
the people's loyalty and their readiness to make sacrifices,
Goebbels, who usually expressed himself in carefully calculated
terms, exploded, saying the people had also failed. "What can I
do," he said indignantly, "with a people whose men don't fight
even when their women are raped!" In the East, he said, "his
face red with fury," the people run away, and in the West they
welcome the enemy with white flags. He had no sympathy for

the German people, especially since they themselves had chosen their fate. During the plebiscite on Germany's withdrawal
from the League of Nations in 1933—a free election—the
people voted against a policy of submission and for a policy of
risk. The gamble just happened to end in failure. Rising from
his chair, he added, "Yes, that may come as a surprise to some
people. . . . Don't harbor any illusions! I didn't force anyone to
work with me, just as we didn't force the German people. They
appointed us. . . . Now their little throats are going to be
slashed!" On his way out, having almost reached the door,
he turned once more and screamed into the room, "But when
we step down, let the world tremble!"

Meanwhile, news had reached the bunker that in addition to
the breakthroughs by Marshal Zhukov in the Middle Sector
and Marshal Konev in the South, the Second White Russian
Front under Marshal Konstantin K. Rokossovski had smashed
through the German lines near Stettin and was advancing on
Berlin. In a typical ploy, Hitler did not withdraw all available
forces to the defensive perimeter around the capital. Rather he
conceived of the Soviet breakthrough as an opportunity for a
powerful counterattack. On his situation map, a little flag bearing the notation "Steiner Combat Group" was stuck into a spot
near Eberswalde. It was from there that he would take the
troops for this counterattack. A new unit under SS General Felix Steiner was to be created by combining the Steiner Combat
Group with General Busse's Ninth Army. They were to break
through the Soviet offensive flank in the southeast and restore
the crumbling front extending from Berlin as far as Cottbus.

Marshal Ivan Stepanovitch
Konev, Zhukov's rival in the
capture of Berlin

"An evasive maneuver toward the west is expressly forbidden,"
Hitler warned. "Officers who do not follow this order unconditionally are to be taken into custody and summarily shot." To
Steiner he said, "I hold you personally responsible for the
execution of this order, or your head will roll."

The problem was that Busse's army consisted only of scattered troops of soldiers desperately battling a direct threat of
encirclement, and there was no "Steiner Combat Group." Even
though all sorts of emphatic commands had been issued, they
were in part contradictory or impossible to carry out because
of the prevailing confusion at the front. Moreover, General
Heinrici, the commander-in-chief, had not been informed about
the plans to create this new unit. As soon as he learned of them,
he got in touch with Krebs.

Operation Steiner, Heinrici declared, was completely hopeless and would endanger his units. He insisted that at the least the Ninth Army, which was now threatened with encirclement, be withdrawn, and he offered to resign if his demand could not be met. He would rather fight as a plain *Volkssturm* soldier, he said, than carry out a command that would only result in the senseless sacrifice of human lives. But Krebs remained adamant, and even when Heinrici pointed out that they both had a responsibility for the troops, he did not change his mind. "It's the Führer," Krebs lectured his caller, "who bears this responsibility."

The following day, when Heinrici and General Alfred Jodl, chief of the Wehrmacht operations staff, arrived at Steiner's command post, it became evident how much more accurate Heinrici's assessment of the situation was. Even before they started discussing what needed to be done, the SS general asked his visitors, "Has either of you actually seen my units?" At the end of the conference, Heinrici mentioned Hitler's attack order, the last sentence of which had been directed at Steiner personally, "The fate of the Reich capital depends on the success of your assignment." Heinrici, apparently appealing to Steiner's high rank in the SS, added, "You have to attack, Steiner—for the sake of your Führer." Steiner stared at him, momentarily stunned, and then burst out, "But he's *your* Führer too!"

The confusion grew by the hour. On the morning of April 22, Lieutenant General Hellmuth Reymann, who had been appointed commanding officer of Berlin at the end of February, was relieved of his post. Hitler and especially Goebbels had often accused him of indecisiveness. His successor was Colonel Ernst Kaether, who had been National Socialist Party leadership officer for the education and ideological supervision of the troops. Now he was unexpectedly promoted to the rank of lieutenant general. But when Kaether spent the rest of the day informing everyone of his glorious appointment and then failed to measure up to high expectations, he was relieved of his post that same evening and demoted to his former rank of colonel.

It was rumored at this time that General Weidling had transferred his command post from southeast Berlin to Döberitz in the western part of the city. When Busse and Hitler found out about the general's unauthorized action, they separately ordered that Weidling be instantly relieved of his command, court-martialed, and shot. But the general, instead of giving in, immediately went to the bunker under the Reich Chancellery. In one of the subterranean corridors he ran into Krebs and Burgdorf, stopped them, and asked why he was to be shot. After he described the situation in his sector of the front, and convinced them that his command post in southeast Berlin

General Helmuth Weidling participated in the battle for the Seelow Heights. On April 22, Hitler ordered him shot for making an arbitrary decision. Yet only a day later he appointed him commandant of the defensive area of Berlin.

"was only a mile or so from the most forward combat line," both generals became "significantly nicer" and decided to accompany him to Hitler's quarters in the deep bunker.

Hitler's "face was puffy" and his "eyes were feverish," Weidling recalled, and when they sat down he was horrified to see that the Führer's left leg, even when he was seated, was "constantly in motion, like a clock pendulum, only somewhat faster." No sooner had Weidling described the situation in his defense zone than Hitler started talking. He was following the execution of the plan for the defense of Berlin with "increasing astonishment," he said; he talked about how the Russian forces would first be "destroyed" in the southern part of the city and how they would then be engaged and "annihilated" by Steiner's, Busse's, and other units that were freed up in the meantime. Simultaneously "other forces" would engage the Russian army in the north, and finally one group would join the other and engage in the decisive battle. Before he left the bunker, Weidling contacted his staff, briefed them on his discussions with Hitler, and passed along some tactical orders. The next day Krebs told Weidling that Hitler had appointed him, Weidling, "Commandant of the Berlin Defensive Sector." "It would have been better if you had ordered me to be shot," the stunned general replied drily, "then this cup would have passed from me."

The surprises did not stop there. One name had come up repeatedly in the preceding days, gaining in importance and engendering the most extravagant hopes. Early in the afternoon, General Krebs called on Heinrici and told him that the Twelfth Army under General Walter Wenck, stationed near Magdeburg, would make an about-face and immediately head for Berlin. Krebs added that the decision seemed to be all the more logical since the American troops obviously considered the Elbe the demarcation line and hadn't attempted to cross the river.

The confidence they felt in deploying the Twelfth Army was to some extent justifiable. It was made up for the most part of battle-tested units that had been reinforced by fresh forces. On the other hand, the various components of this combined force now being sent into action had no experience whatsoever in working together. Even more critical and not considered, or perhaps even suppressed, by the strategists in the bunker world of maps with little flags stuck into them, was the fact that Wenck didn't have a single tank at his disposal and almost no antiaircraft guns to combat the enemy's superior air power. Moreover, two divisions firmly promised to him had so far not arrived—and never would. On top of that, during the last few days the sector of the Twelfth Army had been transformed into a huge caravansary for more than half a million refugees who had been driven to the banks of the Elbe by the Red Army, only to be stopped by the American forces on the opposite shore. Augmented day after day by an endless stream of fleeing people, the refugees formed a sort of advance guard of the millions who, in the coming months, would be driven from their homes, taken to camps, or transported to the East to do forced labor.

But Heinrici did not bother to point out to Krebs the countless difficulties that would delay or even prevent any operative plan from being carried out. While mostly ignoring orders from the bunker, Heinrici focused on having his army groups bypass Berlin in the north as well as the south in order to spare the city a dramatic battle that would clearly be pointless. Instead the units were to advance as far as possible toward the British and American lines. Heinrici called General Busse and ordered him to use all forces fit for action, break through toward the west, and link up with Wenck. When Busse, obedient as ever to the Führer, objected, Heinrici said tersely, "This is an order," and hung up.

All that remained now was pure will and the self-deceptive hope for the collapse at any moment of what Goebbels called that "perverse coalition of plutocracy and Bolshevism." He never tired of saying that all military resistance was aimed at gaining time. And with the brazen audacity on which he prided himself, he spoke about the imminent opportunity to join the Russians against the Western Allies. But all the delusions so assiduously constructed and carefully nurtured were suddenly shattered at the dramatic situation conference on April 22.

The conference began shortly after three o'clock in the afternoon, and with people constantly coming and going it dragged on until eight o'clock that evening. Hitler listened to a report about the Soviets' successful breakthrough north of the Oder front with seemingly stoic equanimity. Others reported that enemy forces had taken Zossen in the south, were advancing toward Stahnsdorf, were operating on the northern rim of the capital between Frohnau and Pankow, and had reached the Lichtenberg/Mahlsdorf/Karlshorst line in the east. Hitler broke the silence that followed with a question about the Steiner Combat Group. At first the generals tried to stall, giving him contradictory information. When Krebs finally admitted that the Steiner attack that was to have turned the tables had never taken place, Hitler brooded for a stunned moment. Then the storm broke.

In an outburst unlike anything those present had ever experienced, Hitler suddenly jumped up from his chair and furiously threw the colored pencils he always carried with him during situation discussions across the table. Then he began to scream. His voice, which had been weak and flat for weeks, once again regained some of its former strength. Struggling for words, he denounced the world and the cowardice, baseness, and disloyalty around him. He reviled the generals, condemned their constant resistance against which he had had to fight; for years he had been surrounded by traitors and failures. While all stared straight ahead in embarrassment, Hitler, gesticulating, cleared a space for himself and stumbled unsteadily up and down the narrow room. Several times he tried to regain his composure, only to erupt again immediately. Utterly beside himself, he pounded his fist into his palm while tears ran down his face. Under these circumstances, he repeated again and again, he could no longer lead; any orders he gave were a waste of his breath; he didn't know how to go on. "The war is lost!" he shouted. "But, gentlemen, if you believe that I will leave Berlin, you are sorely mistaken! I'd rather put a bullet through my head." When Jodl was called to the telephone, Hitler sent the others out of the room, asking only Keitel, Krebs, and Burgdorf to remain behind.

Alarmed by the commotion, those living in the bunker had crowded into the hallways and all the way to the bottom of the stairs. Everyone stood around, speculating. Now and then an anxious silence descended when the place shook from the impact of a shell exploding nearby. Suddenly, according to an eye-

witness report, Hitler, stooped and pale, came out of the conference room and made his way to his private quarters without
glancing right or left. In the confusion that followed, a stunned
Bormann went from person to person, saying over and over,
"The Führer can't have been serious when he said he would
shoot himself." At the same time Keitel urged everyone to "keep
the Führer from going through with it." After the tempest subsided, Hitler asked several of the conference participants to
speak with him one-on-one: Keitel, Dönitz, Krebs, and Burgdorf,
as well as Hermann Fegelein. At about five o'clock he summoned
Goebbels. Bormann asked Goebbels to persuade the Führer to
retreat to his alpine fortress, no matter what. But Goebbels pre-
tended not to hear this "typical Soviet commissar type's" suggestion. There is reason to believe it was Goebbels's offer to face
death alongside the Führer that finally persuaded the still waver-
ing Hitler to stay in Berlin. In any case, after his conversation
with Hitler, Goebbels immediately went to the office across
the hall and informed Traudl Junge, the secretary, that he and
his wife and six children would be moving to the bunker that
very day. In a tone less emotional and more matter-of-fact
than she was used to from his victory speeches, he instructed
that each child would be allowed to take only one toy. They
were not to bother with a lot of pajamas, since such things
would "no longer be needed." Some time later, apparently having regained his composure, Hitler returned to the conference
room. The end had come, he said. It was all hopeless. And
when almost everyone in the room contradicted him, pointing
to the fighting units that were still available—General Wenck's
approaching army, Busse's forces, and not least the army group
operating in the Dresden area under the loyal Field Marshal

Ferdinand Schörner—Hitler shrugged and said, "Do whatever you want. I'm not giving any more orders."

There was a lengthy pause. He would await death in the Reich capital, Hitler added, he would not let himself be dragged elsewhere; he should never have left his main headquarters in Rastenburg in East Prussia. He rejected all objections to his plan. A telephone call from Himmler was unsuccessful in dissuading him, and he flatly turned down a request for a meeting with Ribbentrop. Contrary to his earlier plan, he said, he would not be confronting the Russians, weapon in hand, if only to avoid the risk of being wounded and falling into enemy hands. Moreover, he was in no physical condition to fight. Overcome by the pathos of the moment, he

"Wenck's Army is coming!" was the optimistic rallying cry spread by the government's propaganda experts during the last days of the war. But General Walter Wenck was unsuccessful in drawing up a combat-effective fighting force, and at the end of April the units that were to relieve the capital got stuck near Ferch, southwest of Berlin.

declared he would die on the steps of the Reich Chancellery. Beguiled by this theatrical image, he repeated this sentence several times. As assurance that he would not go back on his word, he immediately dictated a public announcement stating that he would remain in Berlin and would personally take over the defense of the city.

Then, accompanied by Keitel, Jodl, Goebbels, and a few others, he once more withdrew to his rooms. There he sent for his aide, Julius Schaub, and told him to collect his personal papers from the strongbox at the foot of his bed and wherever else they were, take them into the garden, and burn them. Faced with alarming reports that Soviet troops were about to attack the center of the city from all sides, he appointed the highly decorated SS Brigadier General Wilhelm Mohnke, who had been a member of his *Leibstandarte* since 1933, to take charge of the inner defensive sector, the "Citadel." Mohnke was to be under his personal command, entrusted with the leadership of close to four thousand SS men in the city as well as several smaller Wehrmacht and Hitler Youth units. Next he asked Keitel, Jodl, and their staffs to go to Berchtesgaden and, jointly with Göring, make all necessary decisions there. When someone interjected that no soldier would fight for the Reich Marshal, Hitler replied, "What do you mean, fight! There isn't much fighting left to do, and if it comes to negotiating—the Reich Marshal can do that better than I."

At the end, when they were all sitting around, perplexed and exhausted, Keitel made one more attempt to get Hitler to change his mind. For the first time, he said, he was unable to follow one of the Führer's orders; he just couldn't go to Berchtesgaden. But Hitler said he would "never leave Berlin—never!" When Keitel again remonstrated, there was a sharp exchange

SS Brigadeführer General Wilhelm Mohnke, appointed by Hitler on April 22, 1945, as commandant of the "Citadel," the government quarter in Berlin

that Hitler ended by declaring he would no longer listen to the field marshal. But when Keitel nevertheless went on to say that the Führer could not desert the Wehrmacht, Hitler told him to get out. As he was leaving, Keitel turned to Jodl and said under his breath, "This is the final breakdown."

That night Keitel went to Wenck's Twelfth Army command post, which had moved into the Alte Hölle, the head forester's office near Wiesenburg, some thirty-seven miles east of Magdeburg. As soon as the head of the OKW (High Command of the Armed Forces/Wehrmacht) entered the room, he confirmed Wenck's bias against general staff officers. Keitel and his entourage made a rather grand entrance, and no sooner had he lifted his marshal's baton to the edge of his cap in a hasty salute than he got down to business. "Liberate Berlin!" he said. "Turn all your available forces around. Link up with the Ninth Army. Get the Führer out. Wenck, you're the only one who can save Germany!"

Wenck knew that any objection would be both senseless and a waste of time. He replied that he would, of course, do what the field marshal had ordered. But when Keitel drove off at about three o'clock in the morning, Wenck summoned his staff and told them that the Twelfth Army would defy the orders and would not be heading for Berlin. Instead they would attempt to get as close as possible to the Ninth Army. He told them that their assignment was to establish an extended escape route to the west and to keep it open. As for Hitler, Wenck added, "The fate of a single individual is no longer of any significance."

The staggering news of the April 22 conference spread like wildfire. Hewel told Ribbentrop, Jodl told General Koller, Major General Christian told Göring in Berchtesgaden, and Fegelein called Heinrich Himmler at his new headquarters in Hohenlychen, not far from Berlin. The Reichsführer SS, who had long been preparing himself for the expected power struggle over the succession to Hitler, saw the hour of decision approaching. The gist of Fegelein's report was that the Führer had resigned. With his customary subservience, Himmler even now hesitated to make his claim public despite pressure put on him by his advisers, especially since Hitler's opinion of him had plunged. Nevertheless he felt bold enough to put out various feelers about setting up a meeting with General Eisenhower. It was his intention, he said, to convince the American supreme commander that he and his SS could be of use to the Allies; he not only wanted to work out an armistice agreement in the West, but above all he wanted to ask for American weapons to use in the imminent fight against the Red Army. "Then I will still be able to do it," he told those around him, already wondering whether a bow or a handshake would be more appropriate when he met with Eisenhower. Aware of the important game of statesmanship he was about to begin, he added with scarcely concealed contempt, "Everyone has gone mad in Berlin." What he wasn't willing to acknowledge was that the same thing could be said about his own headquarters in Hohenlychen.

FOUR

Finis

Berlin was in chaos. Each morning hastily mustered emergency units set out to reinforce street barricades, dig anti-tank trenches, or build makeshift shelters. Along the city's perimeter were signs that said, "Refugees not allowed in the Reich capital." Nevertheless, endless treks of people with horses, wagons, and cattle streamed through streets still open in the outer districts, often ending up in the middle of the battle zone. Abandoned freight cars loaded with food supplies, reinforcements, and the wounded clogged the train stations. The bombing raids had stopped since the approach of the Soviet Army, but the city was still aglow with fires, and a steady shower of dusty embers and ash particles drifted down, covering house façades, trees, and people with a chalky layer. Russian planes flew low over the city at all hours, and the unnerving howling of the sirens that had been going on for weeks continued, except now they were sounding a "tank alarm"—

a continuous shrill tone. Military vehicles were everywhere, burnt out or abandoned because they had run out of fuel. Soviet artillery, from positions around the perimeter of Berlin, could now reach all parts of the city, sometimes setting entire streets aflame, house by house, before the advance of the infantry. Even burnt-out ruins caught fire again, according to eyewitness accounts.

Every day more factories, workshops, and utility companies discontinued operations. Frequently there was no running water or power for hours at a time. The use of electricity for cooking was forbidden; violators were punished with death. An unbearable stench hung over everything—a combination of burnt flesh and the garbage and rubble piled up on the softened asphalt. In the city center, people stayed for days on end in cellars and U-Bahn tunnels. Those few who risked coming out wrapped their faces in damp cloths to protect themselves against the acrid fumes from burning fires and phosphorus. The challenges of day-to-day survival seemed endless. The last issues of the newspapers and billboards combined strident victory rhetoric with threats, often next to bizarre advice about how to confront the great perils of everyday life. To "improve your protein intake," one of these recommendations read, go and catch frogs in the city's rivers and lakes. The best way to catch them was by "dragging colorful rags along the shallows near the shore."

Everything was in short supply. After they had assembled at their rendezvous points, *Volkssturm* groups were taken to the front by the few buses and streetcars that were still running. Early on, the Russians had seized three weapon and munitions depots in the outlying precincts, and since there was no way to transport supplies from storehouses within the city (in the

The endless trials of survival: This well-known picture, taken after an Allied air raid toward the end of 1943, captures the unremitting hardship experienced by many of Berlin's inhabitants.

Grunewald and the Tiergarten), more than half of the city's defenders were soon marching against the enemy with nothing more than an armband to identify them. They were instructed to arm themselves by taking rifles and bazookas from wounded and dead soldiers on the battlefield. Ignoring the pervasive shortages, Hitler had also ordered all those born in the year 1929 to be called to arms, arms that didn't exist.

Now that defeat was certain, the regime's need for retribution—long concealed under an appearance of legality—burst into the open. The jails were crowded with political prisoners, especially after the large-scale wave of arrests following the July 20, 1944, assassination attempt on Hitler. In early April, Himmler ordered that none of these prisoners should be allowed to live, setting in motion the machinery of death in those areas still controlled by his units. With the approach of the Soviet vanguard, the Lehrter Strasse prison was shut down and a few of the prisoners charged with lesser crimes were released. The rest were informed they would be taken to Gestapo headquarters in the Prince Albrecht Palace, where they would be freed. At about one o'clock that night a heavily armed SS escort set off with the prisoners. After being told they would be taking a shortcut, they were led to rubble-stewn field, and there they were shot, each with a bullet to the base of the skull. Among the murdered men were Klaus Bonhoeffer, Rüdiger Schleicher, Friedrich Justus Perels, and Albrecht Haushofer, all members of the resistance movement.

At the same time Wehrmacht reports on the mood of the people cited mounting levels of depression and a contagious tendency to discuss the most effective way to commit suicide. For example, Inge Dombrowski, a member of the antiaircraft auxiliary, asked her company leader, a young first lieutenant, to shoot her. After long and tortured hesitation, he acceded to her request and directly afterward killed himself. Rumors of the offensive that the Führer was said to have prepared long ago faded. Instead the story making the rounds was that Wenck's army had just arrived outside Potsdam and was ready to deliver an annihilating blow to the Soviets. There was also talk that the Americans had assembled airborne troops on the other side of the Elbe, and that these forces would come to the aid of the Wehrmacht, joining them in fighting the Red Army. But by now hardly anyone believed these rumors and the all-too-transparent propagandistic slogans. For generations Berliners had managed to get through life's adversities with a bitter and fatalistic kind of humor. Now, as the end was obviously drawing near, they reacted with a popular song, "*Davon geht die Welt nicht unter . . .*" ("This isn't the end of the world . . ."). Neighbors meeting on the street whistled the melody to each other. It became a sort of password, just like the phrase "*Bleiben Sie übrig!*" ("Hang in there!").

The signs of disintegration also affected those in Hitler's inner circle. When Albert Speer—full of "conflicting emotions"—returned to the bunker early in the evening of April 23 to say good-bye to Hitler, he immediately became aware of a slight but telltale slackening in discipline: people smoking in the anterooms, half-empty bottles standing around. Only rarely did anyone get up when Hitler entered a room, nor did conversation cease when he passed by.

Hitler himself seemed melancholy but calm, and spoke of death as though it would be a release. Contrary to expectations, he did not flare up when Speer confessed that for months he had not been carrying out Hitler's orders to destroy everything. Rather, he seemed lost in thought, and several times during their meeting his eyes filled with tears. Some hours later, acting as if he had already revealed too much, Hitler bade farewell to Speer with almost contemptuous indifference, as though the architect no longer belonged there. On his way out, walking through the damaged rooms of the Reich Chancellery, which he had built six years before as "the first architectural testimonial to the Pan-German Reich," it suddenly occurred to Speer how much more fitting it would have been if his life had come to a close by a firing squad ordered by Hitler—Speer had anticipated nothing less.

But that very thought revealed how much Speer still shared the bunker denizens' way of thinking. It demonstrated an utter disregard for life, originated by Hitler, and shared by Goebbels, Krebs, Burgdorf, Mohnke, the members of the *Leibstandarte Adolf Hitler,* and the countless battle-obsessed soldiers in encircled Berlin. The British historian A.J.P. Taylor considered it a great mystery why so many Germans fought on unthinkingly in the ruins of the collapsed Reich, long after the eleventh hour. Since the Germans themselves didn't remember, he added somewhat sarcastically, we would never get to the bottom of it.

But the troops in the inner defensive area did not simply go despondently and obediently to their deaths. It is fairly certain that in a strange, confused way, quite a few of them felt a sense of compensation in the final tumultuous days of battle. What helped them to justify continued resistance beyond all reason was not only the deep-seated conviction that great events were always accompanied by death and destruction. It went beyond that: the soldiers saw themselves called on or perhaps raised up to be the participants in the final act of a great historical tragedy. And they had learned that tragedies on such a scale imbued even seemingly senseless deeds and events with a higher meaning. An infatuation with hopeless situations has long been one of the characteristic features of at least one strand of German thought. It is part of a tradition—one which has produced a vast body of literature—that has proclaimed in complex, brooding theories the "German people's historical call to radicalism" and their heritage of "heroic pessimism." Justification for resistance to the very end could even be drawn from Martin Heidegger's writings on "the courage to confront the dread of Nothingness" (*Mut zur Angst vor dem Nichts*).

Many Germans who participated in the bitter, terribly costly battles that were fought among the ruins of the perishing city derived an unprecedented satisfaction from the fighting. "There was a clear-headed energy we had never experienced before," one German officer recalls. "Our struggle was marked by an indescribable toughness, confidence in victory, and readiness to die. . . . Let Zhukov himself come and take hold of the city, it will come at a high price, even if we have to hold out armed only with pistols."

In addition, in the case of the elite units (and not only the SS), one has to take into account their ideological convictions as well as their belief in Hitler and his mission. They were all prepared for desperate situations. The idea of living in an age of "global conflagrations" with their tragic outcomes was, so to speak, part of their basic training. Ever since he came to power, Hitler and his regime had repeatedly boosted the morale of the nation by intentionally launching "life and death" crises. His series of "weekend coups" in the 1930s can be counted among these. But it was the wartime funerals, celebrated with great pomp and ceremony, that brought him and his followers together. For example, after the defeat at Stalingrad, Göring gave a speech that turned into a kind of doomsday celebration. He referred to "the Hall of the Nibelungs, built of fire and blood." And there was Goebbels's call for total war that culminated "in a mood of chaotic frenzy." At no other time did Party leaders expend such inordinate efforts on making Germans feel at ease as they did in the face of imagined or actually threatening disasters.

Then there was the spreading shock of disillusionment. Year after year, up to the final weeks, the regime, with its web of propaganda and lies, had managed to deceive people about the realities of the war, even describing the worst defeats as traps deliberately set for the enemy, who, so the propaganda would have it, were superior only numerically. Now the system of deception unexpectedly broke down. And, as always when veils are torn and reality takes over, a suicidal mood took hold of the nation along with an indescribable fear of the Red Army's desire for revenge. This was based not only on horrific notions about the "barbaric East," but also on dark suspicions about rampages many German units may have engaged in during the campaigns against the Soviet Union. Then there were the menacing images that accompanied the warnings in their own propaganda posters, which were suddenly plastered everywhere.

Hitler was both instigator and captive of this policy of extreme tension, and sometimes it seemed as if he desperately needed to always balance on the brink of the abyss. The rapid victories over Poland, Norway, and France at the beginning of the war gave him only fleeting satisfaction. Perhaps his decision to march against the Soviet Union—a decision made while celebrating his victories in France—was partly motivated by his desire to test fate. Now he had nearly accomplished his goal.

This theme emerged clearly in the last situation conferences at the end of April, during which he kept repeating that, contrary to his earlier intentions, he was going to remain in Berlin and await death in the Chancellery.

He felt strangely fulfilled, in spite of, or perhaps even because of, the *Tatarenmeldungen*—false, invented news reports—that inundated him. Once again he felt the exhilaration of standing with his back against the wall. During one of the conferences, Hitler spoke with scarcely concealed exuberance about an "honorable end" being preferable to "living a few months or a few years longer in shame and dishonor." Another time he described the encircled government quarter as the "last little island heroically defending itself," and he assured those standing around the map table that it was "not a bad ending to die in a battle for the capital city of one's empire." In various remarks he made during the situation conference of April 25, he ran the gamut of emotions—from absolute madness to angry outbursts to resignation:

> "No doubt about it: for me the battle has reached its climax here [in Berlin]. If it is really true that differences have arisen in San Francisco between the Allies—and they *will* arise— then a turning point can only occur if I land a blow against the Bolshevik colossus. At that point perhaps the others will be convinced that there is but one man who is in a position to stop the Bolshevik colossus, and I am that man and the Party and the German State today."
>
> "If fate decrees otherwise," he said later, "then I will disappear from the stage of world history, an inglorious refugee. But I would consider it a thousand times more cowardly to kill myself on Obersalzberg than to stand and die here. Peo-

ple must not get a chance to say, 'You as the leader, the Führer . . .'

"I am the leader, the Führer, as long as I can actually lead. I can't lead by sitting on a mountaintop somewhere. . . . . It is simply unbearable for me personally to allow other people to be shot for things I did. I wasn't born just to defend my Berghof."

In a final overview of his life, which is actually the last political document he produced, Hitler expounded on what he was born to do and why he was called on to take up a historical mission. According to those close to him, after his return to Berlin in February, and again in April, he spent many evenings in the bunker with Goebbels and Ley. Occasionally Walther Funk, Minister of Economics, was also called in. At these get-togethers, Hitler summed up his life in extended monologues, not only reviewing the conditions and chances for success of his policies but also identifying mistakes and errors he had made. Afterwards, one of those present organized his long-winded and disordered flood of words into a readable text.

Hitler never got over the failure of his "royal ideas" envisioning a German-English alliance. For years, he said, he had courted the British Empire, believing that their common interest lay in excluding Russia and the United States from Old World affairs. In this respect he alone was "Europe's last chance." Instead of recognizing this, the whole world had railed against the difficulties caused by such a policy. "But Europe," he added, "could not be won over with charm and persuasiveness, it had to be taken by force." Moreover, the phony world powers, France and Italy, which had been passed over by history, must be forced to give up their outdated power politics.

Everything depended on England, he explained, and England, led by shortsighted and narrow-minded politicians, had failed him again and again. If only Providence could have given the aging and senile England "a second Pitt instead of this Jew-besotted, half-American drunkard" Winston Churchill. Then the island kingdom could have devoted itself with all its might to the preservation and welfare of its empire while Germany could have followed *its* destiny with a free hand. "The goal of my life and the reason for the rise of National Socialism was the extermination of Bolshevism."

As he saw it, the conquest of the East had long been a goal of German politics, and to renounce it would be much worse than the unavoidable risk of defeat: "[We] were doomed to go to war," he declared. From a military point of view, it was his misfortune to have started the war too late; yet from a psychological perspective it had been much too soon. The German people were not yet ready for the great, fateful battle they were entrusted with: "It would have taken me another twenty years to bring a new National Socialist elite to maturity." He didn't have the time. It has always been the tragedy of the German people "never [to] have had enough time." Everything else followed from that, even the lack of inner balance. In the meantime he understood it as his personal "fate, to lead a people more fickle and suggestible than any other," a people as erratic as the Germans who in the past had allowed themselves to be swept along "from one extreme to another" with peculiar indifference.

At the same time, he said, he too had made mistakes, had made concessions that had not been the result of any particular interest or necessity. Objectively seen, he had to count his friendship with the Italian Duce among his biggest mistakes, one that could possibly cost him victory now. His loyalty to Mussolini had kept him from following a revolutionary policy in North Africa as well as in the Islamic world, especially after Mussolini went to the ridiculous lengths of having himself proclaimed "the Sword of Islam" by paid and terrorized puppets. This alliance was perhaps even more disastrous from a military perspective. Italy's entry into the war had presented the enemy with their first instant victories and given them new confidence. Moreover, the utterly "idiotic" invasion of Greece had delayed the start of the campaign against Russia for six weeks and subsequently brought about the winter catastrophe before the gates of Moscow. "Everything might have turned out differently," he said with a sigh. Common sense prescribed a "brutal friendship" with Italy. Instead he had repeatedly given in to the sentiments of being a good ally.

It had been his lack of toughness, Hitler said, that had cheated him out of a sure victory. In his own defense, though, he could say he had waged war against the Jews "with an open visor" and had cleansed "the German *Lebensraum* of the Jewish poison." In everything else he had been too indecisive, as when he hadn't ruthlessly eliminated all the German conservatives, but instead tried to follow a revolutionary policy with these "gentleman politicians"; and when he missed the chance to liberate the workers of Spain and France from the control of "a bourgeoisie of fossils." He should have incited colonial peoples all over the world to revolt—the Egyptians, the Iraqis, the entire Middle East—"the Islamic world trembled in anticipation of our victories." How easy it would have been to stir things up. "Think of the possibilities!" If he was going to fail, he said, he would perish not because of his radicalism but because of his halfheartedness, his inability to carry things through to the bitter end. The insight that he had gained early in his career, and that he had proclaimed a hundred times but never followed up on decisively enough, was nothing less than that "Life does not forgive weakness."

As records of the last situation conferences show, he continued to reproach himself for this failure right up to the end. At the April 27 conference he explained that, during the seizure of power in the months before the death of Hindenburg in August 1934, he had constantly been forced to make compromises. He could have proceeded much more radically, he complained, if it hadn't been for the "clique around this scum" from the past. "Thousands" should have been "eliminated." One gets a revealing view into the real motives of the Hitler regime when Goebbels shared the sentiment that it was regrettable Austria did not resist the 1938 *Anschluss* (Annexation): "We could have smashed everything."

As if this were another cue to reiterate his decision not to leave Berlin, Hitler responded that he was staying in the capital so that he could more justifiably move against all signs of weakness in the future. His rueful remark about the real cause for his increasingly frequent bouts of despondency sounded the same note: "Afterward one regrets having been so benevolent."

FIVE

Banquet of Death

On the afternoon of April 23, a telegram from Berchtesgaden arrived at the bunker. It was from Göring, asking whether Hitler's decision to "remain in fortress Berlin" invoked the edict of June 29, 1941 that named him, the Reich Marshal, successor to the Führer with full powers in case Hitler became incapacitated.

Göring's decision to send the telegram did not come easily. It was preceded by drawn-out deliberations. He asked General Koller, whom he had expressly summoned from Berlin, to tell him about the most recent events in the bunker. And he was quite alarmed when he heard of Hitler's irrevocable intention to stay in the capital, and of the Führer's instructions to Keitel and Jodl the previous evening that from now on all necessary decisions were to be made jointly by them and the Reich Marshal. Göring then summoned his closest advisers to discuss what should be done. All of them, including the Head of the Reich

Chancellery, Minister Hans Heinrich Lammers, agreed that in their opinion this put in force the provision for succession. After many revisions the telegram, phrased with no hint of disloyalty, was finally sent off. It asked for a reply by 10 P.M. and closed with the words: "May God protect you, and I still hope that you will decide to leave Berlin and come here." Even though Bormann, Göring's old adversary, tried hard to make the telegram sound like an ultimatum, Hitler at first remained calm.

Another telegram from the Reich Marshal arrived at about six o'clock that evening. It summoned Foreign Minister Joachim von Ribbentrop to Berchtesgaden the instant the succession decree went into effect. Now Bormann finally succeeded in sending Hitler into a towering rage by declaring that a coup d'état was in progress. Soon Goebbels joined in, speaking of honor, loyalty, war, and death. But these grandiose words only barely concealed his indignation at Göring's attempt to seize the remnants of power Goebbels thought belonged only to *him*. The tussles of the henchmen continued unabated. As usual, Hitler, who had always used these internecine struggles as a means of exercising his power, was soon drawn in. One last time he vented his long-standing anger and annoyance with Göring. In an increasingly vehement outburst he accused Göring of laziness and failure, of having "made the corruption of our nation possible" by the example he set. According to one witness, he called him a "morphine addict," becoming more and more agitated until he ended up crying "like a child."

Finally, when his anger had subsided, Hitler signed off on a radio message drafted by Bormann. It accused Göring of high treason, which, as everyone knew, was punishable by death. He would, however, refrain from taking this extreme step if Göring would resign from all his offices and renounce the right to succeed him as Führer. Then, as so often in those days, he sank back into apathy and remarked contemptuously that nothing much mattered anymore. "For all I care, let Göring handle the surrender negotiations. If the war is lost, it doesn't matter who does it." In justifying himself later, Göring had good reason to refer back to these remarks. But in the angry outbursts of the final hours, such things were no longer important. After a while, his anger flaring up again, Hitler directed the SS commander's office in Obersalzberg to arrest Göring and his staff and to take them to the Salzburg SS barracks.

At the afternoon situation conference the next day it became known that the armies of Zhukov and Konev had linked up southeast of Berlin, closing the ring around the city. Soon thereafter some of their advance guards ran into each other on Kantstrasse and exchanged fire until Konev was officially informed that his rival was to occupy the center of the city. The front now extended unbroken from Zehlendorf to Neukölln. To the north, Tegen and Reinickendorf had already fallen. At the same time Soviet troops began to harry Tempelhof and Gatow, the two airports of the city. In order to keep air connections open, Hitler ordered that the East-West Axis, an imposing avenue he had inaugurated at a splendid military ceremonial a few years before, be turned into an improvised landing strip. He had the ornate lampposts on both sides of the avenue dismantled—against Speer's express wishes. And he informed those present at the situation conference that he was expecting another 150 elite navy men promised by Dönitz, as well as an SS battalion that Himmler said he would provide— a "last reserve."

But at the moment it seemed more important to him to have the landing strip readied so that General Ritter von

Greim, commander of the Sixth Air Fleet, based near Munich, could use it when he came to see the Führer. No one had been able to dissuade him from ordering the general to appear in person. For a few minutes at least, it would lift Hitler out of the gloom of the bunker and give him an opportunity to put on a ceremonial show. While firing slots were still being chiseled into the walls, and armor-piercing guns were being positioned between the Reich Chancellery and Pariser Platz, the bunker shook more and more frequently as Russian artillery shells struck the area.

The next day, Ritter von Greim landed at Gatow Airport in a Focke-Wulf 190 single-seater fighter plane. The baggage compartment had been rebuilt to provide a seat for his companion, the pilot Hanna Reitsch. When he called the Führer Bunker, Greim was told that all the streets leading to the Anhalter train station as well as a stretch of Potsdammer Strasse were held by Soviet troops. Nevertheless, Hitler insisted on meeting with him face to face. He was not told why.

Although there seemed little hope of getting through, the general and Hanna Reitsch climbed into a Fieseler Storch (a small, slow-flying plane adapted for landing and takeoff in restricted spaces) waiting at the airport. After a turbulent flight, during which their plane was buffeted by wild gusts of wind created by the firestorm raging over Berlin, they flew in low over the darkening silhouette of the dying city, landing a short while later at the Brandenburg Gate. Just before touchdown, an artillery round ripped open the floor of the plane and severely wounded Greim in the leg. Bleeding profusely, he was taken to the Reich Chancellery. There he was treated by a doctor and then carried into the deep bunker on a stretcher. Hitler greeted him with, "There is still loyalty and courage in the world!" As

Hanna Reitsch described it, he informed his visitors, in a flat, expressionless voice and with a glassy-eyed look, about the break with Göring, the dismissal of the Reich Marshal from all his offices, and the order for his arrest. Switching to a more formal ceremonious tone, he named Ritter von Greim commander-in-chief of the air force and promoted him to the rank of field marshal. "Nothing has been spared me," Hitler complained toward the end of the meeting, "no disappointment, no treachery, no dishonor, and no betrayal."

Throughout the short, awkward ceremony, "the thunder and crash of artillery strikes was audible," and "even in these rooms" on the lowest level of the bunker, concrete was constantly crumbling from the walls. Sometimes the shelling became so heavy the ventilation system had to be shut off because the smoke and fumes made it impossible to breathe. What's more, for the first time telephone service to the bunker was interrupted, although only for a few hours. An assessment of the military situation could only be obtained by listening to enemy radio newscasts or keeping in touch with contested sectors of the city over the local telephone system. Even so, a report reached the bunker through several channels that American and Soviet troops had met on April 25 near Torgau on the Elbe and, instead of shooting at each other, had shaken hands. It dashed any hope that the Allied coalition would break apart soon. Hitler made an all-out effort to conceal his disappointment, and with the stubbornness he always fell back on during hopeless times in his life, he assured those at the conference that day, "The situation in Berlin looks worse than it is."

Just the opposite was true. Everything was worse than he and the other cave-dwellers in the bunker wanted to admit. Reports that reached them later revealed that more than half of all the buildings in the center of the city had already been destroyed. But it was only now, under continuous shelling by its attackers, that the city literally died. After the capture of Berlin, Soviet General Nikolai Bersarin said the Western Allies had dropped 65,000 tons of explosives on the city in the course of more than two years; whereas the Red Army had expended 40,000 tons in merely two weeks. Later, statisticians calculated that for every inhabitant of Berlin there were nearly thirty-nine cubic yards of rubble.

The major access roads in particular had turned into narrow lanes choked with debris. People bombed out of their homes wandered through the ruins, often slipping into deep craters filled to the top with greenish water. Members of the *Volkssturm*, wearing helmets and wrapped in heavy coats, rifles slung over their shoulders with ropes, walked through the streets, aimlessly searching for their command posts, confused because both the military sector commander and the local Party officials were responsible for their deployment. Often they received contradictory instructions. Fear and panic were widespread in parts of the city already conquered by the Russians as well as those still held by the Germans. The Red Army leadership immediately set up local administrative authorities and began to restore order, at least temporarily, taking severe measures against violators, including their own soldiers. On the other hand, arbitrary and unpredictable arrests and seizure prevailed at the lower levels, made worse in some places by countless rapes committed by Red Army soldiers, who, drunk with victory, assaulted any and every female, from teenage girls to elderly women.

Inside the defensive circle—as always in times of collapse— ugly things were happening as well. Diaries from those days speak of dissipation, mass drunkenness, and hasty erotic excesses. The writer of one entry said he would never forget those scenes: "There are seriously wounded, dying people, corpses everywhere and the nearly unbearable odor of putrefaction. In the midst of all that, drunken soldiers in uniform are lying around tightly embracing equally drunk women." In a restaurant on the Kurfürstendamm another observer came upon a group of inebriated SS officers who "were celebrating the collapse of the world with ladies in long evening dresses." To many people it seemed as though the city's basest elements were brazenly rising to the top. The majority still behaved decently, but greed and meanness were rampant. Pillaging housewives moved through the half-destroyed residential sections under the fire of enemy artillery, collecting abandoned goods—whatever fell into their hands. Here and there, "street courts" were formed that put the women on trial and, without much ado, strung them up on the nearest tree, cardboard signs around their necks reading, "I stole from my fellow Germans."

Others tried more drastic ways to find an "exit from Hell." When he heard that the heads of the regime were about to leave the city, Professor Ernst Grawitz, vice-president of the German Red Cross and "Reich doctor of the SS," sat down to supper with his wife and children. When all were seated, he reached under the table, pulled the pins out of two hand grenades, and blew up his family and himself.

It wasn't only Party adherents of the crumbling regime who chose this way out. Quite a few who had survived the war, but were not able to cope with the collapse of their world and all it stood for, preferred death. Among the many images of unforgettable horror is that of a doctor who, as Soviet troops approached, realized he had only two ampoules of poison left. So he drowned his two desperately struggling children in the bathtub before killing himself and his wife by injection. There are only rough estimates of how many people died in Berlin in the "suicide epidemic" that started in February 1945: perhaps as many as several thousand each month. When halfway reliable data became available again, it was claimed that at least seven hundred people had killed themselves in May alone.

Meanwhile, Hitler clung to the most improbable reports of military successes, such as the news that two transport planes had landed on the East-West Axis. And he built up absurd expectations inspired by all sorts of pipe dreams. The Russians, he said, would "bleed to death" in Berlin, since they had "taken on a huge burden" by occupying a city of four million inhabitants. Any mention of Wenck's name sparked new hopes. In the situation conference on April 27, when one officer firmly assured Hitler, "Wenck will come to Berlin, my Führer," Hitler's euphoric mood returned. "Just imagine," he said joyfully, "when it becomes known that a German army has broken through [the Russian lines] in the west and is in touch with the Citadel, the word will spread through Berlin like wildfire." But right after that, the old hysteria again came to the fore. "We have no oil resources anymore," Hitler said to those sitting around the table. "This is a catastrophe because it makes any wide-ranging operation impossible. Once I'm finished with this business here in Berlin, we'll have to see to it that we get the oilfields back." Later he had several discussions about which decoration General Wenck should receive for his unprecedented plan to "rescue the Führer."

That day, Mohnke reported that six enemy tanks had turned up on Wilhelmplatz, just a stone's throw from the Reich Chancellery, but had been repulsed by tank-destruction troops that

SS Obergruppenführer Felix Steiner, who was supposed to set up a troop unit northeast of Berlin, near Eberswalde. Hitler expected this unit to counterattack the Soviet flank "with full force." But the frequently mentioned "Steiner Combat Group" never existed.

were quickly dispatched there. The day before, the Schöneberg district had fallen in spite of resistance to the death by four hundred barely fifteen-year-old Hitler Youths.

The Soviet units made rapid advances in Berlin's outlying districts, but as they approached the center of the city, the fighting became fiercer and more bitter. Armored spearheads had demolished most of the roadblocks or had simply rolled over them as though they were "made of matchsticks," leaving smaller nests of resistance along the way to be dealt with later by units armed with guns and flamethrowers. But the advance was stopped at the inner defensive ring. In many areas the Russians had to battle their way forward from house to house. The mock-ups of various Berlin streets constructed for Marshal Zhukov so that he could rehearse his conquest of the city proved completely useless. The house-to-house fighting that caused the most casualties occurred in the area around the flak bunkers between Alexanderplatz and the Rathaus, as well as at the Halle Gate. The Red Army liberated many Soviet prisoners of war from various prisons, especially in the northern part of the city. It was easy to provide them with weapons and send them in to reinforce units thinned by casualties.

Simultaneously, a stream of new and increasingly more urgent radio messages went out from the bunker to Keitel and Jodl in Rheinsberg and Krampnitz. They contained orders that all "units stationed between the Elbe and the Oder" must be moved to Berlin; the "attack to bring relief to the capital [is] to be carried out with all available means and with optimum speed." There were also nervous questions about Wenck and Busse, who were not responding to communications, as well as the Holste Corps, which was operating somewhere northeast of the city and whose name had only recently flashed through the phantasmagoria of the bunker like an auspicious star.

No one asked about Steiner anymore. Hitler merely demanded that the SS Obergruppenführer be relieved of his command immediately and that he be replaced by Lieutenant General Rudolf Holste. But his order no longer carried any weight in the Eberswalde zone. Steiner persuaded Holste to let him continue in charge, orders or no orders. Early on April 28, Krebs became even more impatient, telling Keitel "the Führer expects help immediately; at most there are only forty-eight hours left. If no help arrives by then, it will be too late! The Führer asked me to reiterate this."

To emphasize the urgency of the demands from the bunker, Keitel went to see General Heinrici, who, ignoring instructions from his superiors, had ordered the retreat of General Hasso von Manteuffel's tank army. The meeting took place south of Neubrandenburg at an intersection of country roads clogged in all directions by endless streams of exhausted and careworn refugees moving toward nowhere. Heinrici was accompanied by Manteuffel, but before they could all properly greet one another, Keitel—striking his open palm with his marshal's baton to emphasize each word—shouted at the two officers, asking how dared they act without authorization. They had been ordered to remain at the Oder, not to move a single step backward, and to hold the front line by any means. Heinrici tried to explain that he could no longer hold the Oder front with the troops at his disposal. He had no intention of sending his soldiers into a completely hopeless battle. Moreover, he needed new reinforcements, otherwise he would have to give orders to retreat even farther.

Keitel continued fussing with his baton. Heinrici should not count on getting reinforcements, he said sharply, rather he should attack. That was the Führer's order; that was what he had to do. When Heinrici replied that he would not give such an order to General Manteuffel, Keitel stared at Manteuffel, who said, tersely and meaningfully, "Sir, the Third Tank Army obeys General von Manteuffel." Keitel shouted back, "If the troops don't maintain their positions, shoot them. Then they'll hold the line!"

As chance would have it, just then a truck passed, carrying two utterly exhausted air force men. Heinrici ordered them to approach and said to Keitel, "Sir, here is your chance to set an example. Shoot these men." Keitel, taken aback, stammered something about "arrest them . . . court-martial them," and drove off.

At this meeting, if not before, it became evident how far

Heinrici had managed to distance himself from the crazy fantasy world of the Führer and his commands. His sole focus was to save his remaining troops and to protect the civilian population. The next morning, during another phone conversation with Keitel, Heinrici spoke of the responsibility he felt for his troops. Keitel reprimanded him: "You have no responsibility. You only have orders to follow!" The general replied that in that case he had to advise the field marshal that he was resigning his command. For a moment there was an awkward silence on the other end of the line. Then Keitel said, "General Heinrici, by the power vested in me by the Führer, I relieve you of the command of Army Group Vistula, effective immediately. You are to stay at your command post and await further orders."

In the bunker, too, all remaining hopes were dissipating. On the evening of April 28, a rumor spread that the Russians had reached Wilhelmstrasse and that bloody battles were being fought on Potsdamer Platz. A report making allegations against Himmler had been relayed to the bunker, causing great commotion all day. Now it was confirmed by the Reuters news agency: Reichsführer SS Heinrich Himmler had tried to arrange separate negotiations with the western powers through the Swedish diplomat Count Folke Bernadotte, and had even said he was ready to "implement an unconditional surrender."

The news hit Hitler like a thunderbolt. He had always considered Göring corrupt; he described Albert Speer to Artur Axmann as his other recent disappointment, an unpredictable and unworldly artist. Their failure in this time of tribulation was foreseeable. But Himmler's betrayal signified the collapse of a world. After all, Himmler had constantly talked of loyalty and had invoked it as the highest principle of his "Aryan Germanic Men's Order of the SS!"

"Hitler raved like a madman," Hanna Reitsch remembered, describing the scene that followed. "He turned a dark red, and his face became almost unrecognizable." Accompanied by Goebbels and Bormann, he withdrew to his private rooms. When she saw him some time later, "he was chalk-white," and looked "like someone whose life had already been extinguished."

At midnight, still fighting to recover his composure, Hitler went to Greim's sickroom. Sitting on the edge of the general's bed, he ordered Greim, whom he had just named commander-in-chief of the air force, to make his way to Plön in Schleswig-Holstein immediately and prevail on Dönitz to do whatever it took for Himmler to get the punishment he deserved. "A traitor cannot be my successor," he said. "See to it that he won't be." Greim, and later Reitsch, too, argued with him. They had decided to stay in the bunker and die alongside Hitler. Besides, they said, it was now no longer possible to get out of Berlin.

But Hitler was insistent. He had already ordered an Arado 96 (a lightweight two-seat aircraft) for them, he said, and it had landed on the East-West Axis in the middle of the battle melee. He handed Reitsch two poison capsules "in case of an emergency," and then said good-bye. As he was leaving the room he added, "One can already hear German artillery fire near Potsdam." Walking out into the hallway, he expressed his indignation about Himmler to everyone who passed, varying the wording each time. Now he knew why Himmler had failed at the Vistula, why the SS offensive in Hungary had ended in defeat, and why Steiner had refused to follow his order to attack. It had all been betrayal and intrigue. The Reichsführer SS, he said, had even intended to deliver him alive to the enemy. Meanwhile the remaining bunker inmates hastily wrote farewell letters to their families and gave them to Hanna Reitsch, who would perhaps be the last courier to leave the city. Shortly thereafter, in tears, she left the bunker with Greim. Later, describing to General Koller how she felt, she said, "One must kneel with great reverence before the altar of the Fatherland." Once they had managed to get out of the city in spite of all expectations to the contrary, Greim said rapturously that the days spent at the Führer's side had affected him like a "fountain of youth."

At ten o'clock that evening, while the bunker rooms still echoed with loud reproaches of treachery and betrayal, General Weidling turned up for the situation conference. Shattering whatever illusions remained, he reported that the Russians were making "one breakthrough after another," and the defenders had no reinforcements left. In addition, the aerial supply to the city had to be suspended. "Speaking as a soldier," he said, "I think the time has come to risk breaking out of encircled Berlin," so as to put an end to the "incredible suffering of the population."

According to Weidling's notes, before either Hitler or Krebs could react, Goebbels "pounced on me and, using some strong language, tried to make much of my solid presentation sound ridiculous." Krebs left the decision up to Hitler. "After lengthy reflection" Hitler once again stated his objections to demands that the Ninth Army be permitted to break out of its encirclement. In all previous defensive battles, his motto had always been, "Hold out at any price!" A breakout now would be nothing but retreat in disguise. Even if Weidling's suggested plan

was successful, "we would simply end up going from one encirclement to another. Then he, the Führer, would have to wait
for the end out in the open, or in some farmhouse, or something like that."

For the time being at least, Hitler's thoughts seemed to be
elsewhere. Above all, his unbounded rage demanded a sacrifi-
cial victim. Hermann Fegelein's name had come up frequently
during discussions of Himmler's betrayal. Fegelein was a member of Himmler's intimate entourage. The unanimous opinion
was that he was a "thoroughly corrupt character." He had in-
gratiated himself into Hitler's inner circle with a mixture of
charm and unscrupulousness. In the summer of 1944, having
been promoted to lieutenant general of the Waffen-SS, he married Eva Braun's sister Margarete. On April 26 he left the
bunker without explanation and drove to his apartment on
Bleibtreustrasse 4, near the Kurfürstendamm. Two days before,
he had told SS General Hans Jüttner, "I certainly do not intend
to die in Berlin." Now, quite drunk, he telephoned Eva Braun.
As a reputed ladies' man, he had already shamelessly courted
her on the Obersalzberg, and now on the phone he tried to persuade her to leave the bunker. There was no need to think it
over. She must come to him, he said, instead of waiting for certain death in the bunker. "Eva, you must leave the Führer. Don't
be stupid. It's a matter of life and death!"

On April 27, when Hitler wanted to speak to him, Fegelein
was nowhere to be found. He ignored a telephone summons
transmitted by the head of the Reich Security Service, SS
Major General Johann Rattenhuber, to come to the Reich
Chancellery immediately. Members of the Führer Escort (*Begleitkommando*) were dispatched to fetch Fegelein. Bunker gos-

"A thoroughly corrupt character" is what Albert Speer and many others called SS General Hermann Fegelein. Step by step, the ruthless careerist and gentleman equestrian managed to insinuate himself inside Hitler's inner circle. In the summer of 1944 he married Eva Braun's sister Margarete. That did not stop Hitler from having him shot on April 29, 1945. The photo shows Fegelein (*center*) with Margarete and Eva Braun.

sip had it that Eva Braun, who had enjoyed her brother-in-law's advances, had called his apartment on Bleibtreustrasse in great agitation. But all her efforts to get Fegelein to come back were futile. With scornful arrogance, he refused to obey Hitler's first summons. Not until another request was sent, this time by *Kriminaldirektor* of the Reich Security Service Högl, was he persuaded to return to the Reich Chancellery escorted by armed guards of the *Begleitkommando*. They reported they had found him, still drunk, in the company of a young red-haired lady. When Hitler's chief pilot, Hans Baur, reproached him for conduct that aroused suspicions of desertion, Fegelein replied, "If that's all you have against me, go ahead and shoot me."

But it was only the reckless exuberance and foolhardy insolence of a careerist spoiled by success that had prompted Fegelein to say this, so he was surprised when he was demoted even before his first interrogation. When Mohnke told him that he would be stripped of all his medals and decorations, Fegelein tore off his epaulettes, cursing Mohnke and the two SS officers who were with him. He was not answerable to anyone but the Reichsführer, he shouted indignantly, and consequently he would let only Heinrich Himmler interrogate him. He then demanded to be taken to Hitler. But Hitler angrily turned down this request, saying he wanted nothing to do with him. At first Hitler considered handing Fegelein over to one of Mohnke's units. But Bormann and Otto Günsche persuaded him that Fegelein would "just take off" at the first opportunity. Hitler then decided to order a court-martial. Eva Braun begged Hitler to spare her brother-in-law out of consideration for her sister, who was close to giving birth. But Hitler rejected her plea so brusquely that she gave in, saying, "You are the Führer."

The court-martial called by Mohnke had to be interrupted because of the "total inebriation of the accused," and Fegelein was taken back to his cell to sober up. The next day he was "sharply interrogated" in the cellar of the nearby Church of the Trinity (*Dreifaltigkeitskirche*) by Gestapo Chief Heinrich Müller. While the questioning was under way, the news of Himmler's betrayal arrived. Suddenly more was at stake than just the incriminating little suitcase containing jewelry and currency found in Fegelein's apartment. In searching his office in the cellar of the Reich Chancellery, they also found a briefcase full of documents indicating that Fegelein, as Himmler's confidant, knew about the ongoing contacts with Count Folke Bernadotte.

Enraged, Hitler ordered Fegelein to be shot on the spot, without a trial. Shortly before midnight he was taken out of his bunker cell by several agents of the Reich Security Service. Unaware of what was happening and still angrily shouting vile epithets, he was shot, presumably either in the cellar corridor or near the exit to the garden behind the Reich Chancellery. So great was Hitler's craving for revenge that when the execution unit did not return within a few minutes, he asked repeatedly for the execution report. Eva Braun, who had her own reasons for mourning the deceased, said, "Poor, poor Adolf. They have all deserted you; they have all betrayed you."

It was during these hours that Hitler realized he had to bring things to an end once and for all, and as always, once he had made up his mind after long vacillation, he made his decisions rapidly and without hesitation. Around midnight he had the small map room hastily prepared for a civil wedding ceremony. A civil magistrate who had worked in Goebbels's *Gau* (district) office for a while and was serving in a *Volkssturm* unit stationed nearby, was brought over in an armored vehicle and told to marry the Führer and Eva Braun. Goebbels and Bormann were the witnesses. Mindful of the formalities, the couple asked for a wartime ceremony, citing the special circumstances. They then declared they were both of "pure Aryan descent and free of any hereditary diseases."

After the marriage application was approved, the magistrate turned to the couple and asked Hitler and Eva Braun if they were willing to enter into matrimony. When both said yes, he declared the marriage "valid under the law." As they were signing the document, a flustered Eva Braun started to write her maiden name, then crossed out the first letter *B* and wrote "Eva Hitler, née Braun." Afterward, in their private rooms, they were joined for a drink and to reminisce about bygone times by Generals Krebs and Burgdorf, several adjutants including Colonel Nicolaus von Below, and Hitler's secretaries. The news of Hitler's marriage had hardly started to make the rounds when some of those living in the upper bunker decided to follow the Führer's example. In the course of that night, several marriage ceremonies took place at which the state secretary in the Propaganda Ministry, Dr. Werner Naumann, acted as registrar.

Perhaps the incongruous idea of a wedding as a prelude to a double suicide—as though on his deathbed Hitler longed for legitimacy—marks the moment when he finally gave up. He had often explained that as Führer he could not have personal ties to another human being; the monumental conception he had of his role did not allow for images of an ordinary personal life. Now he abandoned this position and with it his belief in

Hitler's marriage certificate
signed by the couple, showing
Eva Braun's "slip of the pen"

the special mission for which he had been chosen by Providence. In fact, he told the wedding guests, the idea of National Socialism was finished, never to be reborn. He was looking forward to death as a release. Then he left the wedding guests in order to dictate his last will and testament.

He drew up both a political and a personal will. The former was dominated by protestations of his innocence and accusations against "statesmen who were either of Jewish origin or worked for Jewish interests," as well as recriminations against the "blind and characterless individuals" who had betrayed their own cause. Once again he justified his decision to remain in the Reich capital, there to "choose death . . . of one's own free will." Under no circumstances did he want to "fall into the hands of the [hated] enemy who needed a new spectacle, staged by Jews, for the amusement of their inflamed crowds."

He named Fleet Admiral Karl Dönitz to succeed him as head of state and supreme commander of the armed forces. Referring to a navy code of honor that ruled out any thought of surrender, he assigned Dönitz the task of carrying on the war even after his death, to the ultimate doom. He expelled Göring and Himmler from the Party and from all their offices, and appointed a new Reich government with Joseph Goebbels as chancellor and Martin Bormann as Party minister. Finally, he appealed to the loyalty and obedience "unto death" of all Germans, and in his last sentence returned again to the obsession that was his wild personal fantasy: "Above all, I call on the leaders of the nation and their followers to scrupulously observe the racial laws and to mercilessly resist international Jewry, the universal poisoner of all peoples."

Hitler's personal testament was much shorter. In it he justified his decision to "take as his wife the young woman who after long years of true friendship voluntarily came to this practically besieged city in order to share her destiny with mine." In addition he listed a few provisions for his estate and named his "most loyal Party comrade Martin Bormann" as the executor of his will. The document concluded with the words "I and my wife choose death in order to escape the shame of deposal and surrender. It is our will that our bodies be burned immediately in the place where I performed the greatest part of my daily work in my twelve-year-long service to my people." That very morning, three messengers were dispatched, each carrying a copy of the marriage certificate as well as Hitler's last testaments. One set was intended for Dönitz, the second for Field Marshal Schörner, and the third for Nazi Party headquarters in Munich.

Just before one of the couriers, Heinz Lorenz, chief of the German Information Office, left the bunker, Goebbels handed him a hastily composed "Addendum to the Political Will of the Führer." It explained why Goebbels had decided to remain in Berlin. For humane reasons, he "would never have the heart to leave the Führer alone in his most difficult hour." In the "delirium of betrayal" all around them, there must at least be a few "who will stand by him unconditionally unto death." He believed he could serve the German people best by acting as a role model. "For this reason I declare, on behalf of myself and my wife and in the name of my children who are still too young to speak for themselves but who, if they were old enough, would join me unreservedly in this decision, my irrevocable resolve not to leave the capital of the Reich, even if the city were to fall, but rather to end a life that no longer has any value for me personally if I cannot risk it in service to the Führer and at his side."

On April 29, a bright spring Sunday, the Northern Command reported that house-to-house combat was raging "day and night" in the center of Berlin. By this time only the area closest to the government quarter, the Tiergarten, a narrow strip of land stretching from the Zoo station west to the Havel River, and a few small defense posts were still in German hands. The report also spoke of "mutinies" in the southern sector, ordered

"the most drastic action" to be taken, and denied a news broadcast on a Munich radio station "that the Führer has been killed
in action." A radio message to Keitel again called for "lightning-
fast and hard-as-steel" action and demanded that "Wenck,
Schörner, and others prove their loyalty to the Führer by
quickly coming to his aid." Somewhat later Krebs got in touch
with Jodl, but the conversation was cut off in midsentence because, as it turned out, the captive balloon that provided the
radiotelephone connection to the bunker had been shot down.

At the midday situation conference, Hitler sent for Wilhelm Mohnke and requested an update on what was happening at the front. Mohnke spread out a map of central Berlin
and reported bluntly, "In the north the Russians have moved
close to the Weidendammer Bridge. In the east they are at the
Lustgarten. In the south, at Potsdamer Platz and the Aviation
Ministry. In the west they are in the Tiergarten, somewhere between 170 and 250 feet from the Reich Chancellery." When
Hitler asked how much longer Mohnke could hold out, the
answer was "At most twenty to twenty-four hours, my Führer,
no longer."

Hearing this, Hitler ordered his dog handler, Sergeant Fritz
Tornow, to poison his German shepherd bitch, Blondi. The animal was not to fall into Russian hands; the very thought of it
made him sick, he said. What seems to have been even more
important was to test the effectiveness of the cyanide that had
been distributed to all in the bunker in the last few weeks. Since
Himmler's betrayal, it could no longer be assumed that poison
obtained from the SS would work instantaneously, which is what
mattered to him. But as soon as Tornow crushed the cyanide
capsule with a pair of pliers, releasing the poison into the dog's
open jaws, the animal fell on its side "as if struck by lightning."

Shortly thereafter, an eyewitness reported that Hitler went to he bunker exit to "say farewell to the dog." When he came back to the deep bunker, another account said, he looked "like his own death mask" and "without saying a word shut himself in his room." Meanwhile, near the garden exit, Tornow shot Blondi's five puppies.

A strange, empty stillness spread through the bunker. Anyone who came to deliver a report or a message left again as quickly as possible. "They were all afraid to stay down there," the bunker telephone operator, Rochus Misch, noted; the atmosphere made you feel "as though you were in a coffin." The usual conference participants sat around and indulged in aimless games of strategy. Hardly anyone believed that regular military operations were still possible. And indeed most of the fighting units, disregarding all orders coming from the bunker, had long ago begun to follow their own judgment in organizing resistance operations.

From time to time those who were not needed would leave the stuffy situation room just to escape the claustrophobic atmosphere. They would head upstairs to the *Vorbunker* or into the cellar of the Reich Chancellery. Meanwhile some of the rooms had been cleared for the Security Company of the *Leibstandarte* and for people from the neighborhood looking for shelter. A larger section was set up as a hospital, to which more than three hundred people, most of them seriously wounded, had been admitted. Two doctors and some nurses and aides hurried through the hallways, caring for the patients. While the doctors performed surgery on blood-spattered tables, the nurses and aides carried the dead, or large tubs filled with amputated limbs, through the indescribably crowded corridors to the bunker exit. Among those in the *Vorbunker* were innumerable Party office holders, administration officers, or high-ranking officials who, because of their loyal service to the regime, felt entitled to special protection in accordance with their rank. These chaotically crowded rooms were the dark backdrop for an "Armageddon," as another report put it, where "everyone was trying to drown their misery in alcohol. The best wines, liqueurs, and food delicacies were brought over from the huge stocks in the Chancellery." Here, too, everyone was talking about "when and how to kill yourself." One of the bunker inmates described himself "as the inhabitant of a morgue" in which the dead were still pretending to be alive.

Suddenly, at about ten-thirty, an orderly came into the conference room. He said he had accidentally tuned in to a short-wave broadcast reporting news of Mussolini's death. Two days earlier, Il Duce and his mistress, Clara Petacci, had been captured in a village on Lake Como. They were unceremoniously shot the following day. But more than anything else Hitler was troubled by what happened next. On several occasions he had expressed fear that the Russians would drag him to Moscow and put him on exhibit in a "monkey cage"—a "waxwork figure" on display for the amusement of the rabble. Now Mussolini's fate reawakened and reinforced this nightmare image. The two corpses had been taken to Milan, and there, at a gas station in the Piazzale Loreto, they were hung upside down while a screaming crowd beat them, spit on them, and threw stones at them.

The news from Italy settled oppressively over all who were waiting aimlessly in the bunker. That evening Hitler—as though he were once again expecting relief for Berlin—sent a radio message to Jodl. It consisted of five desperate questions: "Inform me immediately: 1. Where are Wenck's spearheads? 2. When will they attack? 3. Where is the Ninth Army? 4. Where is the Ninth Army going to break through? 5. Where are Holste's spearheads?"

As hour after hour passed without a reply and any remaining confidence dwindled away, Hitler abruptly got up and went to the conference room to say farewell to his closest colleagues. Goebbels had come over with his wife; Burgdorf and Krebs were there, and so were Mohnke, Rattenhuber, and Hewel, as well as the secretaries, Hitler's diet cook, Miss Manziarly, and several high-ranking SS officers—twenty people in all. Hitler shook hands with each, making a personal comment to one or the other, but with all the noise from the diesel engines supplying the bunker with electricity and fresh air, his words, spoken barely above a whisper, could hardly be understood. Then, addressing the group, he said he did not want to fall into Russian hands and therefore he had decided to commit suicide. Everyone present was freed from his or her oath to him. He hoped they would be able to reach the British or American lines. To Rattenhuber he said he would remain in his predestined place in the Reich Chancellery and would keep "eternal vigil" there.

At 3 a.m., Keitel and Jodl's long-awaited reply finally arrived. It gave four matter-of-fact answers to Hitler's questions: "1. Wenck's spearhead is stuck south of Schwielow Lake. 2. Consequently, the Twelfth Army cannot continue its attack on Berlin. 3. The Ninth Army is fully encircled. 4. Holste's Corps has been forced into a defensive position." One terse sentence was added to describe the hopelessness of the general situation: "Attacks on Berlin have not advanced anywhere."

The next day, April 30, heavy artillery fire woke the bunker inmates at 5 a.m. About an hour later, Mohnke was summoned to the deep bunker. Hitler, wearing a dressing gown and slippers, sat bleary-eyed on the chair next to his bed. He looked up calmly and asked how long they could continue to hold out. Not more than a few hours, Mohnke told him; because the Russians had advanced to within a few hundred yards on all sides, though for the moment their progress had been halted. Hitler commented that the Western democracies were decadent and would lose out to the still fresh and firmly led peoples of the East. Then he shook Mohnke's hand, saying, "Good luck. Thank you. It wasn't only for Germany!"

At seven o'clock, one of the guards noted, Eva Braun came up to the bunker exit. She said she wanted to "see the sun once more," and a little later Hitler himself appeared, a mere shadow in the dim light of the staircase. But when he reached the top of the stairs, the shelling became heavier again, and he turned back and disappeared into the darkness.

Toward midday the situation conference was convened for the last time. General Weidling reported that Soviet troops had launched an assault on the Reichstag and that some of the advance units had already forced their way into the tunnel on Voßstrasse, close to the Reich Chancellery. Situation reports from their own units were no longer coming through, so Weidling, as he had done several times before, had to resort to reports broadcast by foreign radio stations. The city could no longer be defended, he said. Perhaps the Führer should try "to get out of here" and break through to join Wenck's army near Potsdam. Hitler said it was useless: "Anyway, nobody is carrying out my orders." When Weidling asked for instructions in case all their reserve munitions were exhausted, Hitler said he would never capitulate. Wenck and all other commanders were not to surrender. Then he turned and left to attend his final conclave with General Krebs. Only then, when it was long overdue, did he give permission for some units to break out of their encirclement, permission he had refused to give to any unit in recent weeks. A little later the last "Führer command" was delivered to Weidling. It said:

"In case the defenders of the capital city of the Reich face a lack of munitions and supplies, I give my consent for a breakout. They must break out in small groups, and must look for units that are still fighting and join them. If they cannot find any, the small groups are to continue fighting in the forests."

Hitler was the last to leave the conference room when the discussions were finished. He stepped up to Otto Günsche and again emphasized that he, the Führer, must not fall into Russian hands, either dead or alive. He would take his own life, as would "Fräulein Braun" as he characteristically still referred to the woman who was now his wife. He wanted his body to be burned and remain "forever undiscovered." Then he exacted a promise from Günsche to take all necessary precautions when disposing of his mortal remains. Apparently these arrangements were so important to him that he also issued the instructions in writing. Günsche immediately got in touch with Hitler's chauffeur, Erich Kempka, whose office was in the subterranean garage near the Reich Chancellery. Kempka was to go out and get as much gasoline as he could, as quickly as possible; if necessary he could siphon it out of the gas tanks of parked vehicles. When Kempka wanted to know what it was for, Günsche said he couldn't talk about it on the telephone. A little later some SS men arrived carrying several canisters of gasoline, and deposited them in the *Vorbunker*. On their way over they had to duck behind banks of earth and under projecting masonry to protect themselves from a hail of Soviet artillery fire.

At about 2 p.m. Hitler ate his last meal in the company of his secretaries and his diet cook. Contrary to expectations, Eva Braun did not join them at the table. After his numerous emotional outbursts and apoplectic fits of recent days, Hitler appeared to be calm and under control; the little gathering around the table in his living room seemed like "a banquet of death" to one of the secretaries. The evening before, Hitler had given her one of the copper cartridges in which capsules of poison were kept, telling her he knew full well what a miserable farewell present it was.

Not much later Hitler rose from the table and said, "The time has come; it's all over." He then went across the hall to talk to Goebbels. Faced with the inexorable approach of death, the man who liked to refer to himself as the "last of the faithful" put aside his oaths of honor unto death and suddenly urged Hitler to leave Berlin. But Hitler repeated all his old arguments, some of which Goebbels himself had raised. Presumably Hitler also asked him the question he had posed several times recently in rejecting attempts by others to persuade him to escape: After all, where could he go? He did not want to "perish in the streets." Finally he said, "Doctor, you know my decision. And that's that!" Goebbels, on the other hand, might want to seriously consider leaving Berlin with his wife and children. But for once Goebbels refused, swearing he would not leave the Führer's side.

One farewell followed another. Goebbels' wife had joined them in the meantime and Hitler walked the couple to the door. Here he came upon his personal aide, Heinz Linge, who asked if he could say good-bye. Hitler urged him to try to get through to the West with the others. Linge, a simple man, asked him why and for whose benefit he should make the effort. Hitler replied, "For the man of the future." Linge uttered something about loyalty enduring beyond death, and stretched out his arm in a Nazi salute. Hitler then returned to his private rooms.

A little later he walked into the large conference room, his wife at his side. Wearing a simple uniform jacket with the Iron Cross pinned to the left side of his chest, and displaying his decoration for wounds sustained in the First World War, Hitler faced his closest associates, who had lined up for a kind of official good-bye. Goebbels, his wife, and Bormann were at the beginning of the line; then came Generals Krebs and Burgdorf and Ambassador Hewel, as well as the naval liaison officer at headquarters, Vice-Admiral Hans-Erich Voss. At the end of the line were Rattenhuber, Günsche, Högl, Linge, and the secretaries. With his wife at his side, Hitler walked down the line, saying little in reply to the meager formal phrases and breathlessly uttered words that were spoken to him. He disappeared into his quarters while Eva Braun went over to talk to Magda Goebbels for a moment. Meanwhile some SS officers of the Führer's Escort, who had been summoned by Günsche, assembled in the *Vorbunker.*

It is not certain whether Hitler summoned his pilot, Hans Baur, at this time or whether he had already done so before the farewell gathering began. When Baur and his deputy, Georg Betz, entered the room, Hitler grasped Baur's hands, thanked him for his years of devotion, and spoke again about the cowardice and betrayal that had brought him to this end; now he could no longer go on. When Baur made one final effort to

Some members of Hitler's entourage during the final days: (*left to right*) Johann Rattenhuber, SS general and head of the Reich Security Service, a detachment of about 250 men assigned to protect Hitler; Otto Günsche, Hitler's personal adjutant; Heinz Linge, Hitler's orderly; and Gertraud "Traudel" Junge, one of Hitler's four secretaries, who stayed in the bunker to the end

persuade him to escape—there were planes with a range of seven thousand miles standing by to fly him out; they could take him to one of the Arab countries, to South America, or to Japan—Hitler said no, he was putting an end to it all. One had to have the courage to face reality. Tomorrow millions would curse him. But "Providence did not want it any other way."

Then he also asked Baur to do what had to be done to burn the corpses. Under no circumstances must his and his wife's remains be allowed to fall into the hands of those swine, as had been the case with Mussolini. Before they parted, he gave Baur the Anton Graff portrait of Frederick the Great with which he had so often communed in the last few weeks, sitting before it, lost in thought. (One of the bunker telephone operators had once seen him as he sat in his living room with a candle flickering in the draft from the ventilator, staring at the picture in a sort of "trance.") Just as Baur was turning to leave, Hitler returned to the subject he had brought up earlier. The epitaph on his tombstone, he said, should read that he was "the victim of his generals."

But there was to be still another interruption. Magda Goebbels suddenly appeared, "dissolved in tears" and "extremely upset," asking to speak with the Führer. Hitler, though visibly annoyed, was persuaded by Günsche to see the desperate woman. A longtime ardent admirer of Hitler, she had resolved, if the worst came to pass, that she would kill her children before committing suicide. All efforts to dissuade her had been unsuccessful and she had even stubbornly said no when Hitler urged her to reconsider. She could not let her husband die alone, she said, and if she was going to join him in death, then their children must die too. However, she had started to vacillate in the meantime, as had Goebbels. While her husband remained outside the door, she spoke agitatedly to Hitler, urging him one last time to leave Berlin. But Hitler wanted to hear no more. He curtly turned down her plea, and "after about a minute," according to Günsche's report, she "left, weeping." Artur Axmann also came running over and wanted desperately to speak with the Führer, but Günsche pointed out that he had strict orders to let no one in.

As in the days before, an oppressive stillness spread through the bunker. Small groups or individuals sat around, waiting. And then as though this existence, with its penchant for theatrically staged events, could not end without one last absurdly garish scene, dancing began in the *Vorbunker* canteen—the bunker inmates seeking release from weeks of unbearable tension. All the strict rules they had followed for so many years, though visibly neglected recently, now collapsed in an overpowering feeling of relief and finality. Boisterous music came from the loudspeakers, penetrating to the farthest corners of the underground labyrinth. An orderly was sent upstairs to ask for quiet. The Führer, he told them, was about to die. But none of the canteen guests, most of whom were drunk, paid attention to his request, and the carousing continued.

It has not been possible to establish with any certainty what happened next. Some witnesses say they heard one shot at about three-thirty in the morning. After Hitler's farewell, Gertraud Junge, a secretary, had wanted to escape the close, stuffy, and melodramatic atmosphere in the deep bunker. She headed for the upstairs rooms and ran into the Goebbels children, sitting forlornly on a stair landing. She got them something to eat, read them a few stories as a distraction, and tried to answer their fearful questions. Suddenly, she recalled, she heard a pistol shot, and nine-year-old Helmuth cried out in happy excitement, "Bull's-eye!" Other witnesses argued that it was impossible to distinguish specific sounds over the constant pounding of the diesel engines and the humming of the ventilator fans.

Those who had participated in the farewells were waiting with barely suppressed restlessness in the large and small conference rooms. Finally, Hitler's aide Linge, having sought comfort in several hastily swallowed glasses of schnapps in the guardroom, entered the anteroom to Hitler's quarters. According to his account, he immediately smelled gunpowder, stepped out into the corridor, and said to Bormann, "It's done."

Both men, followed by Günsche, went into the adjacent room. Hitler slumped on the flowered sofa, his eyes open, his head bent. A coin-sized hole gaped on his right temple, from which a bloody rivulet had run down his cheek. A 7.65-mm Walther pistol lay on the floor. Next to it a puddle had formed, and the rear wall was splashed with blood. Hitler's wife, wearing a blue dress, was beside him, her knees drawn up to her chest, her bluish lips pressed tightly together. Her pistol, unused, was lying on the table in front of her. The room smelled of gunpowder, smoke, and bitter almonds. Some people who had been in the bunker claimed that Hitler, evidently following the advice of Dr. Werner Haase, one of the bunker doctors, had bitten into a cyanide capsule and at the same time shot himself in the temple—or, as another version had it, in the mouth. On the other hand, SS General Rattenhuber theorized, based on various reports, that Hitler had taken the poison and then had been shot by a third person who was following a standing order. What really happened has by now become impossible to reconstruct.

It was vital to act quickly. Günsche, after a moment of dazed contemplation, went into the conference room, softly clicked his heels, and said, "I must report: The Führer is dead." Goebbels, Krebs, Burgdorf and the others—their faces expressionless—followed him into Hitler's study, where Linge was already wrapping the body in a blanket. Then, with Högl's help, he carried Hitler's corpse past the small group of mourners into the large conference room. As some of those present remembered it, Hitler's legs protruded from the blanket, swinging lifelessly back and forth. Bormann followed, carrying Eva Braun's body.

Goebbels was the first to speak. He would go upstairs now and head for his ministry at the Wilhelmplatz, he said. Then he would walk around until a bullet put an end to his life. Filled with guilt and anxiety, they were discussing what had occurred and what should happen next, when Erich Kempka, Hitler's chauffeur and the manager of the motor pool, barged into the room. Not knowing what had happened, he asked Günsche what all the confusion was about and whether Günsche had "gone out of his mind" in demanding delivery of several canisters of gasoline during such intensive shelling. Günsche, horror still showing in his face, took him aside and said, "The chief is dead." Kempka stared at him aghast. "How could that be?" he shouted, "I talked to him only yesterday! And he was healthy and completely alert!"

After getting over his initial shock, Kempka went to the foot of the stairs and joined the bearers who were taking Hitler's corpse upstairs. Günsche carried Eva Braun's body. They had to stop at the garden exit because gunfire repeatedly drove Linge, Högl, and the others back. Only after several attempts did they manage to put the bodies down on the ground a few yards from the bunker exit. Bormann stepped up, drew the blanket away from Hitler's face, stood there in silence for a few seconds, and then pushed his way back into the group at the bunker exit. Finally, under a hail of splinters and chunks of wall and earth, and in spite of the ongoing shelling and the fires blazing all around, they poured some ten canisters of gasoline over the corpses, lit matches, and tossed them on top. However, in the firestorm raging around them, the matches kept going out. Günsche had brought a hand grenade to get the fire going, but Linge pulled some sheets of paper from the cuff of his sleeve and twisted them into a torch. When the shooting briefly let up, he lit the paper and threw the improvised torch on top of the corpses.

Instantly a mighty tongue of flame leaped up, accompanied by a loud explosion. Everyone stood at attention. Then, still inside the stairwell with the door barely ajar, they stepped forward one by one and raised their arms in the Hitler salute. Black smoke and swirling rubble enveloped the spot where the corpses were burning, and the last thing they saw through the crack in the doorway was the bodies shrinking and limbs jerking eerily in the flames.

Meanwhile Russian troops had attacked the nearby Reichstag and had run into furious resistance. For reasons in some way vaguely related to the Reichstag fire at the end of February 1933 and the subsequent trial of the alleged communist arsonists, Soviet leaders had chosen neither the Reich Chancellery nor the Brandenburg Gate as the "symbol of Berlin," but rather the deserted ruin of the Reichstag on the Königsplatz. While they were still at the Oder, several Soviet units had been given special banners to be hoisted once they captured the "German Kremlin."

Their assault on the building, which was bricked up on all sides, began before dawn. But because of gunfire coming from the ruins of the nearby Kroll Opera House, they could not make any headway. Later that morning the Russians attacked again with a great array of tanks, artillery, and rocket launchers, some of which had been positioned in the upper stories of the Interior Ministry building across the way. But they got no farther than the flooded opening of the railroad tunnel. A renewed attack at noon, following massive preparatory artillery shelling, also failed because of gunfire from the ministry building. The Soviet commanders then decided to await the arrival of darkness. This time a few of the attackers finally managed to reach the steps of the Reichstag, and using two horizontally aimed mortars, they blasted an opening into the masonry. The entrance hall quickly filled up with additional units. Fanning out in the pitch dark, they fought to gain control of the building, room by room and floor by floor.

Not until midnight, Moscow time, was "Banner No. 5" of the Corps of Rifle Guards of the Sixty-ninth Army, which had led the attack, raised on the roof of the Reichstag by an escort of selected soldiers, all members of the Soviet Communist Party. Later it turned out that some Soviet artillerymen had planted a flag atop the building a few minutes earlier. But their feat was declared "unofficial." The staged photo of the flag raising taken in daylight shows the "official" group. A report by the commanding officer, General Semen I. Perevertkin, unrealistically and with some poetic license says, "Not until evening as the sun began to set, lighting up the entire horizon with its red glow, did two of our soldiers raise the banner of victory on the burned-out cupola."

The fighting for the Reichstag actually continued without

The official (staged) photo showing the raising of the Russian flag over the captured Berlin Reichstag, taken by the famous Soviet photographer Yevgeni Khaldei

letup until midday on May 2. It was especially intense in the labyrinthine cellar dungeons, where Soviet troops had to grope their way forward like blind men, often ending up shooting at one another. When the German defenders ran out of ammunition, they fought on in the dark, man to man, with knives, shovels, and gun butts. The clubbing and stabbing went on even after cleanup work had started on the nearby Pariser Platz and Red Army soldiers had begun scratching their names into the walls inside the upper stories of the Reichstag. The Soviet troops finally resorted to flamethrowers to subdue the remaining defenders in the subterranean vaults, while aboveground some German women who had been commandeered moved in to sweep the streets with birch brooms. Only then was the battle over.

But not the war. The Soviet claim that the capture of the Reichstag signified the end of the war may have been valid in a symbolic sense. On April 30, however, when Marshal Zhukov pressed General Chuikov to tell him whether all of Berlin would be conquered in time for the May 1 celebration, he was informed that the continued and unexpectedly fierce German resistance permitted "no hope for a quick capitulation." Once more the strategic mistakes made by the Soviets at the Seelow Heights were exacting their price.

That afternoon Rattenhuber was asked to obtain more gasoline, since the two corpses near the garden exit of the bunker were still not completely burned. As soon as it arrived, the guards poured it over the partially burned cadavers or simply threw the opened canisters from the bunker exit toward the corpses. Early that evening, when SS Unterführer Hermann Karnau went to the spot, he saw only skeletons. When he tried to move them into a hollow in the ground, they disintegrated into a flat pile of ashes, as though touched by a spectral hand. Karnau, still worried, returned to the spot at eight o'clock, but by then, he reported, "flakes of ash were already being blown about by the wind."

The end remains unclear. Günsche said he had assigned an SS officer to remove the remains of Hitler and Eva Braun Hitler. Shortly thereafter he was told that it had been done. But, incredibly, neither he nor any of the other participants personally ascertained that Hitler's personal order for his body to be burnt to ashes had indeed been carried out—not even General Baur, who had promised Hitler he would see to the complete elimination of the corpses. Only Bormann and Rattenhuber, according to an eyewitness account, appeared briefly at the bunker exit after darkness fell. Another witness reported that the ashes were pushed onto a tarpaulin after dark and lowered into a nearby shell crater; some soil was then shoveled in and tamped down with a wooden pole. But no one could say whether the artillery shelling that had continued unabated for twenty hours and the use of flamethrowers by Soviet troops would even have permitted such elaborate measures.

It was reported that when Rattenhuber visited the site of the immolation late that night, he wept and said, "I have served the Führer for ten years, and now here he lies." Indeed, the final break could hardly have been more abrupt. In one of the pathos-heightened images of his death, Hitler had visualized his burial site atop the roof of the bell tower that was to dominate the banks of the Danube in Linz, his hometown. Instead he was buried behind the devastated Reich Chancellery in a wasteland of rubble, tamped into earth that had been plowed up by incessant bombardment, among chunks of blasted concrete and heaps of garbage.

SIX

The Will to Destroy

I t is said that only when a life or a historical phenomenon
ends, can the forces that determined it be clearly understood. Among the questions raised by Hitler's demise was:
When he fired the shot that ended his life on the afternoon of
April 30, 1945, did he see himself as a failure? The answer is by
no means as obvious as it might seem at first glance, and more
thoughtful observers have expressed some uncertainty.

For what happened in the months leading up to May 1945
was more than the unavoidable horror that accompanies total
defeat—cities destroyed, millions of refugees, utter chaos. Rather it
seemed that up to the last death throes of a Reich that had clearly
been defeated, there was a guiding energy at work intent not only
on prolonging the war but on the country's total destruction.

As early as the autumn of 1944, with the enemy approaching
the German borders, Hitler issued a series of orders extending
his scorched-earth policy—which was already being applied in

varying degrees during the German army's retreats in the East and the West—to the territory of the Reich itself. Increasingly emphatic orders went out that all life-supporting installations must be destroyed: industrial plants and public utilities, sewage systems, railway tracks, and telephone lines. All bridges were to be blown up, every farm burned to the ground; even monuments and historical buildings were not exempt. A few months later, on March 19, 1945, in his so-called "Nero Command" descriptively titled "Measures for Destruction Within Reich Territory," Hitler once more publicly confirmed his intention to create "a desert, void of civilization." "All military, transportation, communication, industrial, and public utilities, as well as all other resources within the Reich that could be utilized by the enemy now or in the foreseeable future for the continuation of the war are to be destroyed." Several sets of instructions for the implementation of the order dealt with details.

The demolition of factories, mines, and food warehouses was begun immediately in several locations. Preparations were made to blow up railroad tracks and to block canals by scuttling cement-filled barges in them. The process of evacuating entire cities and regions, begun when American forces first broke through in the West, was accelerated, even though the masses of displaced people wandering about aimlessly increased the confusion in the combat zones and hampered military operations. When one of the generals tried to dissuade Hitler from implementing his evacuation plan, pointing out that it was impossible to move hundreds of thousands of people across the country without any means of transportation, food, shelter, and other essentials, Hitler turned away from him without saying a word. A "flag order" dictated that all male residents of houses displaying white flags of surrender were to be shot on the spot. A decree issued at the end of March ordered that the war was to "be fought fanatically. No consideration can be given to the civilian population at this time."

It would be a mistake to interpret these orders as a last, desperate, defensive measure against the approach of a superior foe. The intent to demolish had always been Hitler's first and preferred course of action, an expression of his true voice, which now could be heard once more. Similar sentiments are expressed in one of the early fighting songs of the emerging Nazi movement, which promised to "smash everything to pieces." After the Nazis seized power, however, this theme was drowned out by slogans about national honor and peace, and then in the early war years by the fanfares that accompanied the special public announcements. In the thirties, some opponents of the regime's domestic policies had already rephrased the refrain of another popular Nazi song to: "Today we destroy Germany, tomorrow the world!" With Hitler's "scorched earth" policy, this resolution once again became a prominent aspect of his thinking.

A profound desire for destruction remained, even behind the strategy of dissemblance that dominated the peaceful years before the war. It could be seen not only in Hitler's constant self-reproach for his many instances of "leniency" and Goebbels's documented expression of regret at not having "smashed it all to pieces." But during the situation conference on April 27, when the conversation turned to the question of how they could do things better after the final victory, the commandant of the Citadel, SS Gruppenführer Wilhelm Mohnke made what may have sounded like a cynical remark: "We haven't quite accomplished what we intended to do in 1933, my Führer." But Mohnke was no cynic, and the situation was not one that

As its rule ended, the Nazi regime did its utmost to ensure that the country would literally perish. The body of a German soldier killed on the steps of the east wing of the Reich Chancellery, early May 1945.

called for scorn or even bitterness. Mohnke, one of the radical praetorians of the regime, was simply expressing the resolve obvious behind all those maxims about the "salvation of the world," namely the boundless destructive drive that motivated Hitler and his sworn followers. Since their rise to power they had needed enemies, had derived their self-assurance from these enmities, had virtually defined themselves by them, and wherever such enemies were lacking they had spared no effort to create them. In that, they certainly hadn't failed.

Hitler wasn't motivated simply by bitterness and terror. In fact, disaster engendered complex feelings of fulfillment in him, which led him to stage the approaching defeat as a historic spectacle of doom. As early as March 1945, Goebbels had told a press conference, "If we go down, then the German people will go down with us, and they will do it so gloriously that even after a thousand years the heroic defeat of the Germans will be at the forefront of world history."

Apart from its theatrical appeal, Hitler and his closest followers were also motivated by their intention to mythologize themselves and their movement worldwide. Like prehistoric tribal chieftains, they sacrificed countless human lives in their death ceremonials. Statistics from the last weeks of the war list on average tens of thousands of victims daily. For example, the commanders of the Ninth Army, which found itself encircled early on, repeatedly requested that Hitler allow them to break out, but found their requests repeatedly rejected until the entire army group was senselessly annihilated at the end of April. Another example, much larger in scope, was the drive toward the East, which grew into "an ideological war of annihilation." Significantly enough, its start was the signal to begin large-scale extermination measures against so-called inferior races—the Slavs and especially the Jews.

The more hopeless the situation, the more drastic were the Nazi regime's actions. Occasionally it attempted to extend the annihilation beyond its own demise. Even Admiral Dönitz, who considered himself an extremely proper if strict commander, did not shy away from praising murderers. In a "Secret Order of the Day" dated April 19, 1945, he assured a navy noncommissioned officer that he "fully appreciated" what he had done and cited him as exemplary: Several German prisoners in an Australian prisoner-of-war camp, where the officer was interned, had indicated that they opposed Hitler. The German noncom had arranged to have them "killed by the guards . . . unobtrusively." Nor was this a unique case. One often gets the impression that with the passage of time Hitler's resolve to destroy increased in scope. In numerous speeches and conversations he spoke of the alternatives facing Germany as either "world power or doom." Actually, there were no such alternatives; there were merely different forms of destruction.

Only a superficial observer would have been fooled by Hitler's fits of despair during the final weeks. The same can be said of his self-deceptive maneuvering—directing ghostly armies that no longer existed, the false declarations of victory, or the frequently expressed hope that his own life would be extended, if only by several days. Such things were certainly at play. But even more intense were Hitler's hatred of the world and his thirst for extermination, which surfaced after the start of the war and were now freed of all constraints. According to a report by Franz Halder, at that time army chief of staff, Hitler had insisted during the campaign against Poland that Warsaw be bombed, even though it was ready to surrender. He had then eagerly watched the annihilation of the city through field glasses, excited by the devastation he saw. Later he debated whether to destroy Paris, Moscow, and Leningrad, and derived pleasure from the thought of the devastating effects a bomb or rocket attack would have on the canyons of Manhattan.

Too many of his destructive impulses had missed their targets. Now at last, with the Reich crumbling, he had the chance to fulfill this deepest need. There's no doubt that the ruin and destruction of those final weeks gave him a greater sense of satisfaction than any of the fleeting victories of earlier days. He reacted to the devastation caused by the Allied bombing campaign by saying that although the Allied bomber fleets had not exactly followed the plans for the redesign of German cities, still, it was a start—and what may sound like irony was deadly serious.

Perhaps he would have liked to stage the final act in a more grandiose fashion, less helpless, more operatic, perhaps with a greater display of pathos, horror, and a more apocalyptic final salute. Still, it was an exit of memorable dimensions. The fame and glory he had sought all his life had never been merely that of a statesman, the ruler of an authoritarian welfare state, or that of a great military commander. There was too much of the Wagnerian in him for any of these roles, too much of a craving for destruction. As a teenager he saw *Rienzi* for the first time from the standing-room stalls in the Linz Opera House. The opera tells the story of a medieval insurrectionist and tribune of the people who is destroyed because of the world's tragic lack of understanding. In the end he chooses death. Even decades later Hitler would joyfully confess, "That's when it all began for

me!" Now, years later, it was ending, and the feelings of exulta-
tion were scarcely diminished.

Hitler not only accepted that in this way he was turning
against his own people, but he embraced it with growing ruthlessness. As early as November 27, 1941, when the possibility of
failure first cropped up with the beginning of the winter catastrophe at the gates of Moscow, he had told two foreign visitors
that the German people ought to "perish and . . . be annihilated"
if they were "no longer strong enough and willing to shed their
own blood to ensure their survival." Nor would he "shed a single tear for them." And on March 19, 1945, "in an icy tone of
voice," he had said to Albert Speer, "If the war is lost, the
people will also be lost. There is no need to be concerned about
the essentials the German people would need to survive at
even the most primitive level. On the contrary, it is better to
destroy these things, to destroy them ourselves. Because the
[German] people have proved they are the weaker ones, and
the future belongs exclusively to the stronger people in the
East. Besides, after this struggle, those who are left will only be
the inferior ones, for the good have fallen."

After Stalingrad and the turning point in the war, all his decisions were marked by an element of disappointed hatred of
the German people. This mindset governed the entire strategy of
the last phase of the war. It began with his repeated refusal to
set up secondary defense lines against foreseeable breakthroughs
by the enemy armies and continued through the Ardennes offensive in December 1944, for which he withdrew strong units
from the Eastern Front so that the "Russian threat" would mobilize the war-weary German people and instill in them the will
to resist. Two years earlier he had said he would, if necessary,
call fourteen-year-old boys to arms because "it would be better

for them to die in the battle against the East than to be tortured in a lost war or maltreated in the basest slavery." Becoming more and more agitated, he said that in spite of all the threats of punishment, the German people in the west were taking down tank barricades and hanging white flags out of their windows. An entire [army] corps had disappeared without a trace. "This is disgraceful!" Whatever was left of his wartime leadership turned more and more into punitive action against his own people. As he had said almost four years earlier, Germany would "perish and be destroyed." He himself intended to do everything in his power to help bring this about in keeping with the "eternal rules" of the struggle for survival.

It was this zealously pursued drive to destroy that kept Hitler going to the end. The appearance of physical frailty noted by all who saw him—the stooped posture, the shuffling gait, and his increasingly feeble voice—presented a paradoxical contrast to his energetic resolve to get things done, as observed by those same witnesses. One of the bunker residents described him as "a cake-devouring wreck," yet still possessed of a hypnotic, unquestioned authority. Gauleiter Albert Forster came to the bunker from Danzig in mid-March. In the anteroom to Hitler's study, panic-stricken and in despair, he described how the Russians had turned up outside his city with a powerful force of eleven hundred tanks, and all the German army had were four Tiger tanks. Danzig, which had been declared a fortress, was utterly unable to defend itself, he said. He planned to explain the hopelessness of the situation to Hitler and force him to come to a clear decision. But after only a brief time in Hitler's study, Forster came out "completely transformed." The Führer, he declared, would rescue Danzig; there was "no doubt about it." SS General Karl Wolff, who had come to the bunker with similar intentions on April 18, was dissuaded from making his plea after Hitler outlined his grandiose plans for the future.

What remains striking is Hitler's political rigidity even as he retained all his powers of persuasion, as well as his inability to think beyond the narrowest military goals. In the 1930s he had scored one success after another with ever-new surprise maneuvers as well as a combination of threats and promises to behave, achieving his first goal in an incredibly short time—the destruction of the European power structure. But by the end of 1937, his behavior signaled that he was tired of these easy triumphs and wanted to return to "the principle" of fighting, whatever the cost. As he boasted in one of his speeches, he had followed this principle all his life.

Even before the war began, Hitler pursued no further political initiatives. At the 1938 Munich Conference he arrogantly ignored the cowardly gesture of appeasement by the Western powers and only acted annoyed because they were spoiling his prospects for the war he wanted even then. Similarly, there were several opportunities to ensure a hegemony over Europe for the Reich, in particular after the victories over Poland and again over France the following year. Yet Hitler did not appear to see the mantle of authority as it came within reach, nor did he ever make a grab for it. It almost seemed as if his military victories were an embarrassment to him because he could not gain anything from a situation without war.

His belief that a prolonged time of peace "would not do [Germany] any good," as he told his generals in August 1939, was presumably also the reason for his complete political abstinence in the years that followed. All advice from those close to him, as well as from foreign politicians like Mussolini, Horthy, and Laval, that he try out diplomatic solutions during the war was rejected. After the turning point in the war in the winter of 1942–43, he repeatedly cited the imminent breakup of the "absurd coalition between Bolshevism and capitalism" as a reason for continuing the war. Only after this coalition fell apart would the time be ripe for fruitful negotiations. But whenever an opportunity arose to widen the split between his enemies, he let it go by. In his diary, Goebbels wrote with annoyance that he repeatedly urged Hitler to act, but one "sometimes has the impression he has his head in the clouds." Based on this, writer and historian Sebastian Haffner suggested that Hitler lacked the constructive imagination of a statesman, and that he had also lost all tactical flexibility, at least from the late thirties on. In his opinion, it was this particular deficiency that caused his failure.

Taking this train of thought one step further, Hitler may well have been little more than a successful gang leader, but one who had at his disposal all the tricks of a reckless streetwise Machiavellianism. The ponderous and anxious politicians on the European scene were no match for him. It was this complete lack of scruples, in his methods as well as in his goals, that for a time helped him achieve his astonishing successes. Like a gang leader, he pursued a course that never went beyond the idea of killing and looting. The conflicts he initiated with growing malice against almost the whole world typically had no particular military goal, and his perplexed generals soon realized this. Other observers saw it somewhat later. In February 1941, when he still nurtured the hope of winding up the campaign against the Soviet Union by autumn, and when he still worried about the prospect of peace, he ordered Jodl to submit a plan outlining an attack against Afghanistan and India.

Anyone who asked him what the war was all about heard

only of his wild visions of "limitless territories," tirades about vast deposits of raw materials, subservient auxiliary nations, and "eternally bleeding borders." Not even in his remarks of February and April 1945, which form a kind of postscript to his vision of imperial power, is there the slightest indication that he ever saw the conquered territories as anything more than areas from which to launch further campaigns. He was tough, insatiable, and without direction, obsessed by the "basic law" of the survival of the fittest, once discarded but now resurrected by him. When his foreign minister tried to persuade him, in the fall of 1943, not to ignore a tentative proposal for peace from Moscow, he shrugged and replied, "You know, Ribbentrop, if I were to come to an agreement with Russia today, I would attack them again tomorrow—I can't help myself."

He wanted to go down in history, Hitler had once said, as a man "unlike any who had ever existed before." The circumstances of his end in that "vault of death," as it was called by one of the bunker inmates, the futile commands and fits of rage with which he tried to ward off the approaching defeat, give the impression that he recognized his utter failure. But going down in style, he believed, made up for a great deal and could also be fulfilling. Typically the last expression of Hitler's will, once again revealing the ruling drive of his life, was an order to destroy, namely the instructions he issued at noon on April 30 that his corpse be burned.

SEVEN

Capitulation

During the evening of April 30, after the corpses were burned and the ashes buried, the now leaderless group of regulars gathered in the bunker for a lengthy conference. After some back and forth, Bormann suggested they make a mass breakout with the help of several hundred members of the *Leibstandarte* who had been detailed to protect the Reich Chancellery. But Mohnke said such a venture was utterly absurd and doomed to failure. Finally they agreed they would first enter into negotiations with the Soviet High Command. General Krebs would go to Tempelhof to see General Chuikov.

Krebs left at about 2 a.m. that night. An hour and a half later he arrived at the private apartment on Schulenburgring where Chuikov had taken up quarters. The Soviet Commander had not anticipated the Germans' sudden offer to talk, and had had no time to call his staff together. Instead he decided to present as his personal "war council" two writers with whom he was about to have dinner, his adjutant, and several junior-grade officers. Also there as a guest was the composer Matvej I. Blanter, who had been commissioned by Stalin to compose a symphony about the capture of Berlin. But when it turned out that Blanter did not have a uniform and therefore could not be passed off as a Red Army officer, Chuikov simply shut him into an armoire in the meeting room and ordered him not to make a sound.

After a few introductory remarks, Krebs came to the point: The general was the first foreigner to be confidentially informed that Hitler and his wife, to whom he had only just been married, had committed suicide in the bunker under the Reich Chancellery. Chuikov had never heard of a bunker on the grounds of the Reich Chancellery, nor did he know anything about Eva Braun, and he certainly had not been informed of Hitler's suicide, but he acted unimpressed and claimed he already knew all about it. Krebs then read him a statement prepared by Goebbels. It listed the order of succession Hitler had drawn up and then raised the subject of "peace negotiations between the two countries that had suffered the greatest losses in the war."

Chuikov did not hesitate a moment. He curtly rejected the all-too-transparent and belated attempt to divide the Allies by means of a separate peace agreement. Some stalling ensued while Marshal Zhukov, who was in Strausberg, was informed. He, in turn, had to wake up Stalin, who also rejected all bipartite deals. Krebs's proposal for a temporary cease-fire was turned down as well; only the unconditional surrender of Berlin or of the Reich could be discussed.

As in every tragedy, the element of comic relief was not lacking. After being locked in the closet for several hours, immobile as though frozen in place and forgotten by all, Blanter suddenly fell out of his hiding place with a loud clatter, landing unconscious on the floor of the conference room. He was taken into one of the adjacent rooms, and the negotiations continued without a word of explanation. There was a protracted argument when Krebs pointed out that he could not comply with the demands for surrender without first consulting Goebbels and Dönitz. He was handed a sheet of paper listing, in five sentences, the Soviet conditions: "1. Berlin surrenders. 2. All those surrendering must lay down their weapons. 3. The lives of all soldiers and officers are to be spared. 4. The wounded will be cared for. 5. There will be an opportunity to negotiate with the Allies by radio." If these demands were not met, Chuikov added, the fighting would resume immediately and with all due force. Almost twelve hours later, Krebs returned to the Reich Chancellery.

Goebbels was indignant. Years ago he had captured Berlin, fighting against the Reds, he said, and he would now defend the city against them "to my last breath. I will not use the few hours I have left as German Chancellor to put my signature on a document of surrender."

Hans Fritzsche, one of the highest-ranking officers in Goebbels's ministry, listened to the distraught men in the bunker, all talking at the same time and agreeing on only one thing—to break off all negotiations and take no further steps—and decided to make a surrender offer of his own.

He went to his office on Wilhelmplatz and composed a letter to Marshal Zhukov. But before he finished it, General Burgdorf suddenly stormed into the room. Drunk and shaking with rage, he asked whether Fritzsche really intended to hand the city over to the Russians. When Fritzsche said yes, Burgdorf shouted

A Red Army soldier directing traffic in the streets of Berlin on May 1, 1945, even as the fighting in the city continued

that he would have to shoot him then because the Führer's order forbidding surrender of any sort was still in force. Moreover, he said, Fritzsche was a civilian and had no authority to negotiate. With an unsteady hand Burgdorf raised his pistol, but the radio technician who had taken him to Fritzsche's office, and was waiting in the doorway, knocked the gun out of his hand. The bullet hit the ceiling. Moments later, several ministry employees overpowered Burgdorf and took him back to the bunker under the Reich Chancellery.

Fritzsche immediately sent two members of his staff through the lines and over to the Soviet side. Not much later he himself followed. Few developments could give a better picture of the confused situation in the city—where spotty fighting continued with undiminished intensity—than the agreement Fritzsche quickly reached with the Soviet High Command: Although he had no official authorization, he was to announce on the radio, in the name of the German government, that the Soviets had accepted Germany's capitulation. In addition, he was to issue an order to all German forces to cease fighting and to surrender, giving up their weapons and equipment and turning themselves in as prisoners of war.

In the meantime, the commandant of the city of Berlin, General Weidling, had also decided to put an end to the now senseless bloodletting. So as not to provoke protests in the bunker, he had told only a few confidants what he was about to do. He was familiar with Goebbels's point of view, and as he was leaving General Krebs had said to him, "There are no desperate situations, only desperate men."

On the evening of May 1, Weidling ordered his troops to stop fighting. A few minutes after midnight he transmitted a radio message to the enemy lines: "This is the Fifty-sixth German Tank Corps. This is the Fifty-sixth German Tank Corps. We ask that you cease your fire. At 2:50 Berlin time, we will dispatch truce delegates to the Potsdam Bridge. They will be carrying a white flag in front of a red light. Please reply. We are waiting."

Shortly afterward the other side replied: "Understood. Understood. Sending your request to chief of staff." After another brief delay, Chuikov radioed his agreement, and at the specified time Weidling, accompanied by three staff officers, arrived at Schulenburgring. When Chuikov asked where Krebs was and whether he had been briefed, Weidling didn't know what to say. When asked whether his cease-fire order had reached all units, Weidling said he had no way of communicating with individual units, especially the smaller ones, and furthermore the SS units were not under his command. Presumably, he added, the fighting would continue in some places because Goebbels had ordered that news of the Führer's death be kept secret for the time being, to keep up morale. Chuikov asked him to draft an order of surrender, but Weidling refused. As a prisoner, he said, he could not issue orders. As the argument raged on, he collapsed from nervous exhaustion, but as soon as he came to, it was agreed that an appeal would be read over loudspeakers wherever fighting was still going on. Weidling wrote the text:

> Berlin, May 2, 1945. The Führer committed suicide on April 30, 1945, thereby abandoning all who swore loyalty to him. In obedience to the Führer's order, you German soldiers were ready to continue the fight for Berlin even though your ammunition was running low and the situation as a whole made continued resistance senseless. I am ordering an immediate halt to all resistance. Every hour you continue to fight pro-

longs the terrible suffering of Berlin's civilian population and of our wounded. By mutual agreement with the High Command of the Soviet Army, I order you to stop fighting immediately. Weidling, former Commandant of the Defensive Sector of Berlin.

Only with this announcement did the disorganized pockets of resistance—operating much like the *Freikorps* after 1918—get their signal to surrender. The day before, Goebbels and Bormann had finally notified Dönitz of Hitler's death. On the evening of April 30 the admiral had been told that he had been named to succeed the Führer in place of the deposed Reich Marshal Göring, information both incomplete and misleading. Actually Hitler had transferred to Dönitz only the office of Reich President and the position of commander-in-chief of the Wehrmacht, not that of Chancellor. Goebbels and Bormann had intended not only to keep Hitler's death secret as long as possible, but, by issuing the misleading information, to perpetuate the internecine power tussles within Hitler's entourage. Both were afraid that Himmler, who had also escaped to Schleswig Holstein, could make use of the fact that Goebbels, in Berlin, was virtually unable to act and insist that Dönitz appoint him (Himmler) Chancellor. But Goebbels and Bormann calculated the admiral would not give up the office as long as he considered himself Chancellor, appointed by Hitler.

After the radio message was transmitted, Goebbels busied himself with the few remaining tasks of the chancellorship. He talked to several people, signed documents, and then—in a sort of stock-taking—withdrew to finish the diary he had been keeping for many years. In a seven-page tract, he tried to justify the policies he and Hitler had pursued over the years, policies for which he had masterfully advocated.

About an hour later, Goebbels stepped out of his room and handed the manuscript to his state secretary, Werner Naumann, asking him to see that it got out of Berlin and was preserved for posterity. But posthumous publication of the tract was not to be. Naumann claims he lost the seven pages in the confusion of his escape. It is not difficult, however, to reconstruct the contents of the manuscript in outline form from the texts that Goebbels had been composing for many years and on which he had been working even more assiduously in the last weeks of his life.

He probably began with the series of justifications he had always used to support the regime's actions, starting with its intention to defend European culture, and a condemnation of the West, which, out of blind hatred for the Reich, had denied all the deadly dangers that were threatening it and had handed the Old Continent over to the Asiatic hordes. Then he would have gone on to criticize those in his own ranks who were not only weakened by the continued betrayal of the old castes, but had been incapable of waging all-out war. All this would have been accompanied and intensified by images of a world struggle between the satanic powers of the abyss on one side and the armies of order and justice on the other, with Hitler as Commander-Savior. Once again, he would have resorted to the religious terms and metaphors with which he, almost twenty years earlier, had given rise to the myth of the Führer, ultimately making it all-powerful. As before, he might then have blasphemously concluded that once Europe had turned Bolshevik, people would longingly remember the Führer because he had once more taken the road to Golgotha, giving his life to save the world.

That evening, Magda Goebbels went to her apartment in
the *Vorbunker*. She had met several times with Dr. Stumpfegger, Hitler's personal physician, and Dr. Kunz, adjutant of the
SS Medical Administration, to learn how to kill her children
quickly and painlessly. She had also given Hanna Reitsch a letter to take to Harald Quandt, her son by a previous marriage,
in which she attempted to justify her decision. She had decided, she wrote, to put an end, "the only possible, honorable
end," to her National Socialist life. And, she continued, "I
want you to know that I stayed with Papa against his will, that
as recently as last Sunday the Führer still offered to help me get
away. But I did not have to think twice. Our glorious idea is in
ruins, and with it everything I have known in my life that was
beautiful, admirable, noble, and good. After the Führer and
National Socialism, the world won't be worth living in, and
that is why I have brought the children here. They are too good
for the life that will come after us, and merciful God will understand if I myself give them deliverance." It was "a merciful
stroke of fate," one she had never dared to count on, that she
and her family and the Führer could end their lives together.

In a brief postscript, Goebbels wrote that he and all the
other Nazi leaders wanted to set an example for Germany in
which it could find new strength to get back on its feet after
surviving the terrible war. His stepson should not let the "noise
of the world" confuse him: "One day the lies will crumble and
the truth will triumph. That will be the hour when we will
tower over everything, pure and spotless. . . ."

On the evening of May 1, Magda Goebbels put her children
to bed, having first given them a sleeping potion; they may also
have been given a morphine injection. Then, in the presence of
Dr. Stumpfegger, with someone holding the children's mouths

open, she put drops of hydrogen cyanide down their throats. Only her oldest daughter, Helga, who in the last few days had been anxiously asking what would become of them all, appeared to have resisted. The bruises on the body of the twelve-year-old girl seemed to indicate that the poison was not administered without the use of force. Magda Goebbels, ashen-faced, came back to the deep bunker where her husband was waiting for her. "It is done," she said. Together they went to his living room, and there, weeping, she played a game of solitaire.

Later, Bormann and Artur Axmann came in, and Magda Goebbels invited them to stay, saying, "Let's sit together one more time, the way we used to during the years of struggle." They sat around the table and exchanged memories of the days when they were still dealing with weak opponents, when they had great expectations. Now and then they were interrupted by a bunker resident coming in to say good-bye. Earlier, Goebbels had exacted a promise from his adjutant, SS Hauptsturmführer Günter Schwägermann, to see to it that his and Magda's corpses would be burned.

At about 8:30 p.m. Goebbels suddenly got up and went over to the coat rack. He put on his cap and pulled on his gloves, and without saying a word, he and his wife walked past a few people who were standing around, and then over to the stairs leading up from the bunker. Magda Goebbels was wearing the golden Party badge Hitler had given her three days before. Only once, when they were already at the foot of the stairs, did Goebbels speak. He told his telephone operator Rochus Misch that he didn't need him anymore, adding "*Les jeux sont faits.*"

When they reached the exit, the couple paused imperceptibly before stepping outside, into the glow of fires blazing on all sides. When Schwägermann, who was still in the stairwell,

Joseph Goebbels and his wife with their six children who were later killed by **Magda** Goebbels in the bunker. Also shown is Harald Quandt, Magda's son from an earlier marriage. Quandt survived. By April 1945 he was a prisoner of war.

thought he heard a shot, he signaled to some SS men who were standing by, and together they carried several canisters of gasoline up the stairs. Since Goebbels had asked him to make sure that he and his wife were dead before they set them afire, Schwägermann summoned a guard, who fired one or two shots at the corpses lying near the exit. Then several orderlies doused the bodies with gasoline and set them on fire. A hissing ball of flames immediately enveloped the bodies, but after a few minutes the fire went out. Everyone was so busy with his own plans to escape that no one bothered about the half-charred remains in the garden of the Reich Chancellery.

After those who were still in the bunker put a few things in order, burned the most important files, and provided themselves with what they would need in their flight, they assembled in the *Vorbunker*. Mohnke ordered that the Führer Bunker be set on fire so that these rooms, which had not only been the central command post of the Reich during the past few months but also Hitler's private dwelling, would not pass intact into the hands of the enemy. Schwägermann and several SS men fetched some more gasoline, poured it about in Hitler's study, and lit it. However, since they had shut the airtight steel door when they left the bunker, and the ventilation system had been turned off, the fire could not spread, merely charring some of the furniture and leaving numerous scorch marks.

Meanwhile, Mohnke assembled the commanders of all units stationed in the government quarter and informed them of the most important developments of the past few hours: Himmler's betrayal and the execution of Fegelein; Hitler's marriage to Eva Braun, their subsequent suicide, and that of the Goebbels family. He told them about the failed attempts by Wenck, Steiner, Holste, and Busse to come to the aid of Berlin, as well as about the fruitless negotiations between Krebs and Chuikov. The assembled officers were stunned; until then they had heard of these events only piecemeal or as rumors. Mohnke told them that City Commandant General Weidling had ordered the fighting to stop one hour before midnight, and sent them back to their units. All forces, he added, should try to get through to the north and, if possible, to reach the area controlled by the Dönitz government.

Shortly before eleven o'clock that evening, the exodus of the bunker residents began. Krebs and Burgdorf stayed behind. Mohnke had formed ten groups of twenty or more people each. Allowing an interval of a few minutes between the departure of each group, they crawled out of the cellar window under the Führer's balcony in the Reich Chancellery, crossed the devastated Wilhelmplatz, which was lit up as bright as day by many fires, and disappeared, slipping and stumbling down the rubble-heaped entrance of the Kaiserhof U-Bahn station. They then walked along the tracks, more or less directly below the Russian lines, toward the Friedrichstrasse station, and from there through the U-Bahn tunnel under the Spree River; their intention was to reach the Stettin station. The weak beams of the flashlights some were carrying fell on dead bodies, the wounded, and those who were seeking shelter there, crowded together against the tunnel walls or huddled on the crossties. Parts of uniforms, gas masks, ammunition cases, and piles of garbage were scattered everywhere. A sidetracked subway car had been equipped as a medical aid post near the Stadtmitte station, and a few doctors were caring for the wounded and the dying by candlelight.

Mohnke led the first group, which included Günsche, Hewel, Voss, and the secretaries. Rattenhuber was in charge of the second group. The third, which included Hitler's pilot Hans Baur and Martin Bormann wearing an SS general's uniform, was headed by Naumann. That morning Bormann had informed Dönitz by radiogram that he would be coming to join him "as quickly as possible." Hitler's chauffeur led another group composed mostly of rank-and-file soldiers and Chancellery staff members, about a hundred people altogether. The original plan to stay in contact soon turned out to be unworkable. The groups lost touch right after entering the U-Bahn tunnel, and not much later the individual members also got separated in the dark underground passage. Those who tried to reach the outside by one of the station exits were driven back into the tunnels by nonstop shelling and showers of rocks. The plan, as it had previously been formulated, was to get through the Russian lines, and once they reached the northern part of the city, to join a unit that was presumably still fighting either on the outskirts or in Oranienburg. But under the circumstances, this scheme turned out to be utterly absurd.

In the course of their wanderings, some members of the groups met up again here and there. At about 2 a.m., Bormann, looking exhausted and irresolute, was spotted on the stone steps of the entrance to a house on Chausseestrasse. Others made their way along paths winding through the rubble, via connecting cellars, and across rear courtyards to the Schultheiss Brewery on Schönhauser Allee, which had been designated as a temporary meeting place. Many died in the house-to-house fighting that was still raging, or in street battles, where it was often tank against tank. Högl and Hitler's second pilot, Betz, were killed at the Weidendammer Bridge; Walter Hewel committed suicide in the Weddinger Brewery, perhaps to keep a promise exacted from him by Hitler.

A larger group that included Mohnke and his staff, as well as Günsche, Baur, Linge, Rattenhuber, and Voss, were taken prisoner by the Soviets the next day. Others, among them Axmann, Schwägermann, and the bunker secretaries, succeeded in getting through to the west. When the Russians occupied the Reich Chancellery, they found General Burgdorf and General Krebs in the deep bunker, sitting at a card table with quite a few half-empty bottles in front of them. They were dead. Martin Bormann was presumed missing for a long time. But soon after the end of the war, there were reports that he and the SS physician Dr. Stumpfegger had committed suicide near the Lehrter train station. In the early 1970s the discovery of some skeletal remains confirmed this. Later these remains were cremated and eventually scattered over the Baltic Sea.

Despite Weidling's call for a halt in the resistance, fighting continued in several parts of the city all day on May 2 and even the following day. But the fires went out or were smothered by the black clouds of smoke rising from the ruins everywhere. Because of downed telephone lines, some officers had not heard the news of the surrender. Others relied on the last order they had received, which called on them to hold their positions at any cost. "Proclamations" and hearsay meant nothing to them; as soldiers they needed orders.

Some doomed units—a few thousand soldiers altogether—considered all negotiations to be "treason" and were determined to fight on. On May 2, one of these units blew up the tunnel under the Landwehr Canal in which countless wounded and civilians had sought shelter. But a major catastrophe was averted because the torrents of water that were released drained off

On May 2, 1945, while fighting continued in isolated parts of the city, the Soviet poet Yevgeni Dolmatovski addressed a group of Soviet soldiers in front of the Brandenburg Gate.

quickly. People said that even nature was tired of the constant killing.

Elsewhere in the subterranean tunnels, a combat unit brought light guns into position and fired off all their remaining ammunition at the attacking Soviet troops. A group of SS officers demanded that the canteen where they were quartered hand over its entire stock of liquor; then, quite drunk, they reportedly ran "under the treads of [enemy] tanks." On the day Soviet troops captured Berlin, an eerie thing occurred. That morning, buildings and walls still standing in the vicinity of the Reich Chancellery were found to have been draped with swastika flags. At first it was suspected that a secret, possibly communist, resistance group, wanted to help the conquerors by marking the target of all their battles. But it turned out that the commandant responsible for that area, twenty-seven-year-old Colonel Erich Bärenfänger, had discovered a storehouse filled with Nazi flags and had decided to show the enemy that he and his men were ready and willing to die. "We fought under this flag in good times," the highly decorated young officer said. (He had been promoted to major general by Hitler in late April.) Why should "I be ashamed to display it now that things are getting rough for us." A few days later, to escape the disgrace of being taken prisoner, Bährenfänger and his wife killed themselves.

A few cut-off or decimated SS units formed a combat group and tried to break through the Russian lines. Among the most determined defenders of the city were the remnants of the French SS division Charlemagne. They fought relentlessly, primarily in the sector where the Air Force Ministry was located. Dutch and Scandinavian SS units and a Latvian corps that by now was whittled down to scarcely one hundred men also put up a desperate suicidal fight, partly because they had never taken any prisoners and were now expecting the same fate.

Most people avoided the areas where fighting was still going on. No one dared to go out on the streets after dark. Nights in the shattered city were filled with frightening noises: the distant rumble of heavy guns accompanied by lightning-like flashes, the sudden racket of revving motors, sporadic bursts of machine-gun fire, and the screams of women nearby. The corpses of soldiers and civilians were lying in the ruins by the hundreds, but no one paid any attention to them.

Anyone who had a choice in the matter considered the war over. Occasionally one saw forlorn Wehrmacht soldiers smashing their rifles against the curbstones, tossing their hand grenades randomly into the ruins, or tearing the ignition cables out of abandoned vehicles. For days afterward, façades of houses would suddenly collapse, as though touched by an invisible hand. Gradually the outer city districts, which had been captured days before, started coming back to life. Exhausted and marked by their difficult struggle to survive, people returned to the streets carrying suitcases or backpacks containing a few rescued possessions. Party badges, pictures of Hitler, and swastika flags disappeared from view. Few believed the news that Hitler had killed himself, since the official report, which said that he died "fighting Bolshevism to his last breath," was more consistent with the widespread public perception.

A sort of disorderly camp life developed in the conquered sections of the city where fighting was no longer raging. Patrolling Red Army soldiers wearing earth-brown jackets marched through the streets, past burnt-out or still smoldering ruins. Smoke would darken whole sections of the city for days to come. Bivouacked Soviet troops, female soldiers among them, were camped in many of the city's squares. They posed for photographs before burnt-out or overturned tanks or trucks, cracking their leather whips on the pavement. Elsewhere, long lines of prisoners waited to be in-terrogated, even while gunfire still flashed in the distance. As they were advancing, the Russians had requisitioned entire herds of cattle. These animals were now standing around waiting to be slaughtered and roasted over open fires while groups of soldiers danced and sang. And everywhere there were small Russian carts drawn by shaggy steppe ponies or dog teams and hung with cheap booty: pots and clothing, watering cans, accordions, dolls, or whatever else the Soviet soldiers had helped themselves to. And in the midst of all this, grim-faced motorized couriers criss-crossed through the crowds. Signs with Cyrillic writing went up at every major intersection.

Meanwhile, prisoners poured into designated assembly points day and night. Worn-out and bone-tired, some with white arm-bands, they came up from the cellars, from holes in the ground and sewer tunnels. Among them were many old *Volkssturm* men, as well as fifteen-year-old antiaircraft helpers, along with the wounded on crutches or wearing blood-soaked bandages. They fell into line silently and then moved off, part of a great gray le-gion, driven forward and escorted by triumphant Soviet soldiers, many of whom were already decorated with medals. When dark-ness fell, the searchlights were turned on. Troop carriers and trucks pulled up on the arterial roads, their headlights switched to bright, flooding the scene with an eerie light. Along the sides of the roads, in the shadows of the ruins, small groups, mostly older women, watched dejectedly as the endless columns of prisoners approached, plodded past, and finally disappeared again in the distance.

When news of the German surrender reached Moscow, an ecstatic victory celebration broke out. Huge crowds filled the streets, shouting, throwing their hats high into the air, embracing. The Great War had been brought to an end, although with immense casualties. The battle for Berlin alone had cost the Red Army 300,000 dead. Some 40,000 German soldiers had been killed. Almost half a million were taken prisoner. There is no reliable figure for the number of civilian victims.

Shortly before midnight, twenty-four salvos thundered from more than three hundred cannons into the Moscow night sky, followed by spectacular fireworks. The city was celebrating the "historic conquest of Berlin." The noise lasted for days, and could be heard in the cells of the Butyrka Prison, to which Weidling, two of his staff officers, and several former bunker residents had been taken as part of the first prisoner transports. Among the inmates was a *Volkssturm* private who aroused the suspicions of the Soviets because his name was Trumann, a name much like that of the new American president. But this Trumann was a cigar-store owner from Potsdam.

The Red Army occupied the Reich Chancellery shortly after 3 p.m. on May 2, encountering little resistance. Contrary to many accounts, the Chancellery was not taken by storm. According to "official" sources, the first Soviet soldier to enter the bunker was First Lieutenant Ivan I. Klimenko, who was subsequently named "Hero of the Soviet Union" for his brave deed. But, as was the case in the capture of the Reichstag, an

After the fighting ended,
huge gray armies of German
prisoners of war were marched
eastward through the ruins
of Berlin. According to Soviet
estimates, they totaled
almost half a million men.

"unofficial" version of events differs from the idealized one in two ways.

At about nine o'clock that morning, Johannes Hentschel, chief engineer in the deep bunker, who had stayed behind, heard women's voices coming from the connecting tunnel. Stepping out of the master control room to investigate, he was surprised to see some twelve women in Russian uniforms who, it soon turned out, were members of a Red Army medical corps unit. Hentschel could tell from their excited chatter that they weren't going to do him any harm. One of the women, evidently the leader of the group, turned to him and asked in fluent German where Hitler was. But her next question, about "Hitler's wife," made it clear what she and her companions were after. They asked Hentschel to lead them to Eva Braun's dressing room. There the women ripped open the closet and the big dresser and stuffed anything that looked usable into some bags and sacks they had brought with them. The engineer reported they came out a little later "howling with glee" and waving "at least a dozen brassieres" as well as other lace-trimmed lingerie. They left in high spirits.

On their way out, the women passed two Soviet Army officers who had just arrived, but who took no notice of them. The officers also asked Hentschel about the whereabouts of Hitler and listened with interest to his description of the marriage of the Führer to Eva Braun, the couple's suicide, and the burning of the corpses. They then had Hentschel show them the rooms of the Goebbels family. But after only a brief look at the dead children, they shut the door, horrified. Later it turned out that they were probably members of Marshal Konev's units, whose advance Stalin had stopped a few days before because Berlin was supposed to belong to Zhukov. These two incidents revealed too much human weakness and unauthorized behavior to be included in the "History of the Great War of the Motherland." Consequently, neither incident ever turned up in Soviet descriptions of the battle for Berlin.

With the capture of the Reich Chancellery, there began a drama of obfuscation and confusion—not without occasional burlesque touches—that not only fooled the outside world for quite a while, but also perpetuated the fiction that Hitler was still alive. In addition to finding innumerable dead bodies in the garden area of the Chancellery, the conquerors also came across the largely burned and disarticulated remains of some fifteen human beings near the bunker exit. Possibly with the help of a makeup artist, they prepared one of these corpses— still in relatively good condition—to look like the dead Hitler. The body was placed among nicely arranged clumps of rubble, and on May 4 it was presented to the general public as a spectacular trophy. Shortly thereafter, however, the Russians quashed the sensation they had created, at first referring to the body as a Hitler "double," and eventually calling it a hoax. Apparently they were trying to decide whether to identify another corpse obtained elsewhere as the body of the German dictator, but one of the experts they consulted realized in the nick of time that the man was wearing darned socks. This would certainly have raised doubts about the identity of the corpse. Somewhat later they spread rumors about yet another find. But because of the earlier mishaps, they did not officially declare it to be Hitler's remains. "The dead body," it was said, "had been lying on a blanket that was still smoking. The face was blackened by fire, the skull pierced by a bullet, but there was no doubt that the horribly distorted facial features were definitely those of Hitler."

At the end of May, Stalin got involved, and the finding of new Hitler doubles suddenly stopped. During a visit to the Kremlin by an American government delegation that included Averell Harriman, Harry Hopkins, and Charles Bohlen, Stalin said he suspected that Hitler was by no means dead but had escaped and, along with Bormann and General Krebs, had gone into hiding at an unknown location. Every so often Stalin would come up with a new version of the German leader's whereabouts. Once he said that Hitler had escaped to Japan in a submarine; another time he mentioned Argentina; and later he said something about Franco's Spain. With the release of each new theory, eager newspaper reporters would pass off one version or another as the definitive if not quite incontestable one.

The tendency to believe in conspiracies, backroom wheeling and dealing, and dark machinations was deeply rooted in the Soviet regime, and the story of Hitler's mysterious disappearance provided fertile ground for speculation. Soon there were ample demonstrations of this. It was claimed that Hitler had made all his faithful followers take an oath to tell the world that they had personally seen how his body and that of Eva Braun were placed on a funeral pyre and burned. Another time it was reported that he had ordered his retinue to erase all traces of his whereabouts. It was also said that at dawn on April 30 a small plane with three men and a woman on board took off on the East-West Axis in the direction of Hamburg. Allegedly originating from secret service sources came word that just before the capture of Hamburg by British forces, a mysterious submarine had put to sea for ports unknown. And so forth.

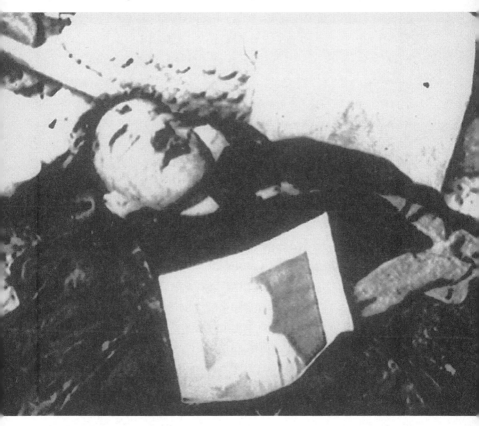

One of the many corpses found on the grounds of the Reich Chancellery. In early May the Russians claimed it was Hitler's body. Actually, on his orders, the dictator's corpse had been cremated on the afternoon of April 30 and, it can be reasonably supposed, was destroyed but for a few remains.

From then on and into the 1990s, the tabloid press in the West took up this tempting and lucrative subject, finding ever new details to report: Hitler, disguised as a woman, had been seen in Dublin some time after his alleged death. The London *Times* reported he had planned to end his life in a sensational *coup de théâtre*, boarding a plane filled with explosives and blowing himself up over the Baltic Sea. Elsewhere journalistic inventiveness drew once again on Stalin's distortions, with the "disclosure" that Hitler had spent the last years of his life under the simpleminded cover name of "Adilupus" in the "Presidential Palace of the fascist Franco" and had died there of "heart failure" on November 1, 1947.

The truth, or what was verifiable, was forgotten in the process. Toward the end of April 1946, a Red Army commission arrived at the garden exit of the Führer Bunker. It intended to establish the facts in the case clearly and unequivocally, and to put an end to all the transparent farces that had created so much confusion for everyone, including the Soviets themselves. Its members brought along a few bunker survivors who had been picked up during the capture of the city. Film cameras were set up, and the cremation of the bodies of Adolf Hitler and Eva Braun was re-created in detail. But this material, as well as information based on the endless interrogations of Günsche, Linge, Rattenhuber, and others, has disappeared into some secret archive—unpublished and never used.

On Stalin's orders, no further use was to be made of the alleged remains of Hitler, Eva Braun, and several other bunker inmates, since Stalin had said they had escaped. Consequently they were buried toward the end of May 1945, on the grounds of the Office of the Department of Counterintelligence in the Berlin-Buch district. When the unit moved, the wooden boxes containing the remains were taken along, first to Finow, from there to Rathenow, and finally to Magdeburg. In response to an inquiry, the Politburo of the Communist Party of the Soviet Union decided in March 1970 to dig up the remains "in strict secrecy" and to "destroy them forever by burning them." The final report on "Operation Archive" says, "The remains [were] completely burned during the night of April 5, 1970. Then, mixed with pieces of coal, they were crushed into powdery ashes and thrown into the river."

The question remains: What was in the wooden boxes that eventually arrived in Magdeburg? The most likely hypothesis is that, in spite of extensive efforts, the Soviet Department of Counterintelligence never found the corpse of Adolf Hitler or that of his wife. This assumption is supported not only by the testimony of the bunker guards who claimed that on the evening of April 30, 1945, they had gone back to the spot where the bodies were burned to bury the ashes, but also by the fact that the Reich Chancellery and its gardens were subjected to intense shelling for more than ten hours after Hitler's death. The high-explosive shells plowed up the earth repeatedly, and the exploding incendiaries, after hitting their target, started devastating fires. In all probability, all this destroyed the last recognizable remnants of the bodies. The only objects found in the rubble that could be definitively identified, according to dental experts summoned to examine them, were parts of Hitler's dentures and "Eva Braun's lower bridgework."

The claim that the corpses were never found is further substantiated by the fact that the Soviet Investigative Commission did not publicly exhibit the remains of Hitler and his wife, even though they did display those of Josef and Magda Goebbels. Fritz Echtmann, a dental technician who was kept in a Soviet prison for several years as a witness, testified that in May 1945 Soviet investigating officers had shown him "a cigar box" in which, besides Hitler's teeth and Eva Braun's bridge, were an Iron Cross First Class and the golden Party badge that Magda Goebbels had last worn. Presumably the badge was found during the days when intensive searches of the rubble around the bunker exit were being conducted, and was declared to be the Führer's Party badge. The cigar box contained—it can be assumed with some certainty—all that remained of Hitler.

EIGHT

The End of a World

It is one of history's paradoxes that Hitler's almost traceless disappearance was instrumental in providing him with a bizarre afterlife. Several generations after his death, his presence has not been erased, and as time passes, he may even be gaining in influence.

What makes Hitler a phenomenon unlike any other in history is that his goals included absolutely no civilizing ideas. Despite their obvious differences, conquering world powers—ancient Rome, the Holy Roman Empire of the German Nation, Napoleon's France, and the British Empire—have all held out some promise to humanity, no matter how vaguely defined, relating to peace, progress, or freedom. Even Stalin's bloody despotism draped itself with promises for the future, extremely threadbare though they may have been. In this way they received a certain exoneration from history, and in the end were often acquitted of charges that greed and thirst for glory were the major motives in their attempts to subjugate other peoples.

Hitler, on the other hand, as he conquered territory and extended his control, rejected all idealistic trimmings, deeming them unnecessary to disguise his claim to power. The German people, who had always prided themselves on discovering the underlying ideas or principles at work in every historical event, were not following an idea or principle when they granted power to the Nazi regime. As a common saying of the day had it, the German people just couldn't think of anything to say when it came to the subject of Hitler. All attempts to ascribe an epochal role to him remained utterly unsuccessful. Though many considered him strange at times, it was Hitler and Hitler alone who carried the masses along, overwhelmed them, and held them spellbound for much too long. The boundless force that drove him throughout his life was the maxim of the survival of the fittest. From start to finish, it alone describes what he propounded as his philosophy of life.

A number of concepts that Hitler acquired early, and to which he clung rigidly and tenaciously throughout his life, grew out of this Darwinist principle. They were aimed at suppression, enslavement, and "racial cleansing," and in the end always left "scorched earth" behind. At no time and in no place did he leave any doubt that he had come as an enemy and intended to stay as an enemy—even in those countries that had at first greeted his troops as liberators. Almost all previous world conquerors had intended to keep subjugated populations in doubt as to whether resistance against the invader was a good thing or would only stand in the way of progress. In Hitler's case, all those who resisted could be sure they were

right to do so. He had said early on that his program was "a declaration of war . . . against any and all existing worldviews."
In his *Table Talk* and *Monologues in the Führer's Headquarters* in the early 1940s, Hitler explained what he meant. Here he spoke more openly than anywhere else, taking every opportunity to mockingly denounce morality, religion, and all humanitarianism. In the real world, he declared, more "naked" laws applied. He dismissed as "priests' twaddle" the rules and regulations that had grown out of centuries of tradition to protect one human being from another. It wasn't only out of deception and cowardice that they had come into being, he claimed; they had more to do with the "original sin" of the betrayal of Nature. And this betrayal, this violation, was nothing less than a revolt "against Heaven." In breaking these rules, one does away "not with the law, but only with oneself." Following this "iron law of logic," he had denied himself all feelings of sympathy when it came to the harsh suppression of resistance inside [Germany] as well as resistance by "foreign races." "Monkeys put to death any members of their community who show a desire to live apart," he explained in the Führer headquarters on May 14, 1942. "And what applies to apes, applies to men, too, at a higher level." No tyrant ever went this far back—to behavior that precedes civilized thought—to justify his ideas.

After Hitler's death, several days went by until Germany's total unconditional political and military surrender. Not only was fighting still going on in some areas, but the Dönitz government, in order to give the greatest number of soldiers and civilians a chance to reach areas occupied by the Western powers, decided to delay things by a process of partial capitulations.

Total capitulation occurred in Reims the night of May 7 at the American headquarters of General Eisenhower, Supreme Commander of the Allied Forces, following a partial German surrender to Field Marshal Montgomery of the British armed forces. It was agreed that hostilities would cease at midnight on May 8. Since Stalin insisted that his top military officers be present, the surrender ceremony was repeated at Soviet military

May 8, 1945: The unconditional surrender in Berlin-Karlshorst by Field Marshal General Wilhelm Keitel, Supreme Commander of the Wehrmacht, who brought his marshal's baton and was wearing his golden Party badge; to Keitel's right, General Hans-Jürgen Stumpff, representing the Luftwaffe; to his left, Admiral Hans Georg von Friedeburg, Supreme Commander of the Navy

headquarters in Berlin-Karlshorst. Members of the German delegation had to wait in an adjacent room during the negotiations, and were only brought in when it was time to sign the documents. General Keitel showed up carrying his marshal's baton and wearing a golden Nazi Party badge. When a member of his staff heaved a sigh during the short formal ceremony, the field marshal barked, "Stop that!"

Assisted by the Soviet military administration, life gradually returned to the ravaged city of Berlin. Recovery teams searched through the vast heaps of rubble for corpses, transporting them in wheelbarrows and carts to the mass graves that had been dug in many places. Demolition squads poked through the debris, looking for mines planted in the final hours of the war. Other teams removed huge chunks of rubble from the debris-littered streets to make them passable, if only in a makeshift way. Sections of some streets had collapsed into subterranean tunnels. Until the end of June, human and animal corpses could be seen floating in the lakes, rivers, and canals of the city. When Harry L. Hopkins, adviser to two American presidents, came to Berlin and saw the extent of the devastation, he was shaken. It's another Carthage, he said. Berlin remained the center of attraction on "grand tours" of the sites of destruction for many years.

As agreed with the Soviets, the Western Allies moved into Berlin in early July. On the sixteenth of that month, one day before the Potsdam Conference was to begin, a grim but proud Winston Churchill visited the city. He viewed the still-imposing ruin of the Reich Chancellery and had a Soviet guard lead him to the garden exit near the place where Hitler's body was burned. Churchill then asked to see the deep bunker where Hitler spent his final months, and followed the Red Army soldier down one flight of stairs. But when he was told there were two more flights, he shook his head and turned back. He wasn't about to subject himself to being holed up that deep underground. Nor did he ask what life had been like down there. Once back aboveground, he had a chair brought out and sat down for a few moments, lost in thought. Then, without saying a word, he got into his car and, accompanied by his personal physician, was driven to Potsdam.

Hitler's Reich ended in a confused series of events, presenting more contradiction, delusion, and drama than many a work of fiction. Though much occurred that was both terrible and tragic, it would be hard to speak of these events as a classic tragedy. For that, at least when it comes to the leading charac-

Marshal Georgi K. Zhukov during the victory parade in Berlin

ters in the final act, there was too much devotion and blind subservience at play. During the April 22 conference, none of the bunker officers ever considered taking Hitler at his word when he said the war was lost. Instead, Keitel, Jodl, Krebs, and others all desperately urged him to continue the senseless fight. Likewise, after Hitler's suicide, none of the high-ranking military leaders was prepared to raise the white flag. To the contrary, they kept the Führer's death secret in order to shore up the German people's will to resist for a few more hours. They even accepted the fact that Zhukov and Stalin were informed of the dictator's death before Admiral Dönitz, Hitler's successor.

It was a submissiveness that recognized no principles— a submissiveness beyond comprehension and beyond all sense of responsibility. Instead, what dominated the entire sequence of events and cost countless lives was an undeterred will, locked in its own mad, delusional world on the one hand, and a deeply inculcated obsequiousness on the other. There were some exceptions, but history—not without a certain logical consistency—gave these individuals only minor roles to play. Others stood in the limelight, bowing and scraping and repeating the same servile lines. But in genuine tragedies there are no roles for servants. The same applies to the theater of world history.

An examination of Hitler's thoughts and actions quickly reveals the profound nihilism that governed his ideas. Almost three years to the day before his death in the Berlin bunker, he had implored those sitting around the table with him in the Führer Headquarters to devote all their efforts to achieving victory; their great opportunity must not be squandered. Then, with a dismissive gesture, he added, "You always have to keep

Victor's spoils: A Soviet soldier carrying a bronze head of Hitler, early May 1945

in mind that if we lose, we lose everything." He knew he had burned his bridges to the rest of the world. But in a twisted way he saw the horrendous shock waves he had initiated as a positive accomplishment. The consequences didn't concern him. Apparently those close to him and many of his contemporaries felt the same way at first. In any case, they believed that once dead, Hitler would be gone from this world. On the evening of April 30, after Hitler's corpse had been reduced to a pile of ashes, Hermann Karnau, a member of the Reich Security Service, returned once more to the tower near the garden exit behind the Reich Chancellery where Rottenführer Erich Mansfeld stood guard. Karnau told him he was no longer needed, he should come down: "It's all over now."

Actually nothing was over. The world gradually became aware of the irretrievable losses Hitler's rise had wrought. What was lost was far more than the devastation visible to all: the dead, the mountains of rubble, and the trail of destruction extending across the continent. Perhaps a world had been lost. For whenever an empire falls, the losses are well beyond what is visible to the eye.

BIBLIOGRAPHY

This volume contains no footnotes. Every citation or incident mentioned can be traced to a source, however. I decided not to use footnote references because of the hopeless confusion in the statements and testimony of the witnesses, much of which can no longer be cleared up. Too often a reference would have to be compared with one or more differing statements or descriptions.

I have already mentioned in the Foreword the many contradictions that exist in the accounts about an event as important and memorable for those directly involved as Hitler's suicide. Witnesses could not even agree upon whether Hitler was found sitting on the sofa next to Eva Braun or on the adjacent armchair when his valet Heinz Linge and Martin Bormann, closely followed by Hitler's personal aide Otto Günsche, entered the Führer's living room on the afternoon of April 30, 1945. The confusion is compounded because the same people sometimes gave different accounts of an event at different times. For instance, the place where the reception for Hitler's fifty-sixth birthday was held, and the sequence of events there remain uncertain; the same goes for the exact order of events at the dramatic conference on April 22. There are many other examples. For the most part the differences concern only minor details. Still, the chronicler must be aware of them and must note even the smallest discrepancy. So as not to burden this volume with an unwieldy apparatus of footnotes, I have used the version given by the most credible witnesses, or the account that seems closest to what probably happened. Nevertheless, wherever doubts arose with regard to the more important questions, I have mentioned that in the text.

In view of these circumstances, it is surprising that when this volume was first published in Germany, hardly any objections worth mentioning were raised by living witnesses. One letter I received noted that Göring had not personally blown up his hunting lodge, Karinhall, but that this was done later by a unit that had remained behind. Another correction comes from one of the soldiers who had been assigned to defend the Berlin Reichstag building. He states that the bitter fighting inside the Reichstag described by all Soviet sources did not take place. Of course, it cannot be ruled out that Red Army soldiers involved in the capture of the Reichstag may have felt obliged to pay tribute to the myth of the dramatic battle for the "German Kremlin." It is also conceivable that the former Wehrmacht soldier who contacted me was deployed in a section of the sprawling building that fell into Soviet hands more or less without a fight.

It may be useful for me to precede the bibliography that follows with a few remarks.

The earliest published account dealing with the final phase of Hitler's life appeared in the summer of 1946 under the title *The Last Days of Hitler.* It was written by the British historian Hugh R. Trevor-Roper, and is based on numerous interviews with witnesses conducted by the author in the summer and fall of 1945. By that time, many potential informants were already in Soviet captivity; others had gone into hiding. Trevor-Roper managed to track down a few of these. Nevertheless, his account unavoidably contains some gaps as well as intentionally misleading information given to him by some informants. Verification by means of comparisons with the statements of third parties was scarcely possible in those days. But these relatively minor flaws in the book are fully compensated by Trevor-Roper's superb overview, his sound judgment, and his splendid style.

Not until almost twenty years later were more comprehensive accounts published. Unlike Trevor-Roper's portrayal, they take up the chronology of the story weeks or months earlier. In addition, they include information contained in numerous memoirs and records (G. Boldt, K. Koller, E. Kempka, E.-G. Schenck, H. Reitsch, et al.) that were not available to Trevor-Roper in published form, and that sometimes broaden the picture with informative details. Then, in the 1960s, four journalists with a historic bent felt challenged by the uniquely dramatic material at just about the same time.

The first of these was Erich Kuby, who wrote *Die Russen in Berlin 1945* (*The Russians and Berlin, 1945*). Prior to its publication in book form, some of the material appeared as a series of articles in *Der Spiegel.* Kuby was followed a year later by the American Cornelius Ryan, who had already written a highly successful account of the Normandy invasion. His work was titled *The Last Battle.* Shortly after that, *The Last 100 Days* by John Toland, another well-known American reporter, was published. This was followed by *The Battle of Berlin 1945* by Tony le Tissier. All these books are based on extensive interviews with eyewitnesses in addition to the various memoirs that had become available in the meantime.

The great readability of these works overshadowed what they lacked in accuracy and especially in historical depth. Much more rewarding is *Die Katakombe: Das Ende in der Reichskanzlei* (*The Catacombs: The Last Days in the Reich Chancellery*) by Uwe Bahnsen and James P. O'Donnell, published in the mid-seventies. It is based on more recent interviews with surviving witnesses and surpasses all the previously mentioned titles in vividness and scope.

Over the years, as is usually the case, various errors have crept into descriptions of the final phase of the Third Reich, and have been passed along from one book to the next. For the most part this was due to contradictory statements often made by those involved. It is to Anton Joachimsthaler's credit that he corrected these inaccuracies as far as possible in his book *Hitlers Ende: Legenden und Dokumente* (*The Last Days of Hitler: The Legends, the Evidence, the Truth*). With extraordinary though occasionally somewhat tart pedantry, he has compared the various findings, determining what seems to be more or less confirmed and weeding out the rest. His documentation, however, is limited to the layout of the Führer Bunker, the death of Hitler, and the still not completely clarified question regarding the whereabouts of the remains of Hitler and his wife.

The present volume, which is concerned above all with what happened in Berlin, draws on information in numerous journals, diaries, and memoirs. Special acknowledgment and particular credit go to several compilations, above all Peter Gosztony's *Der Kampf um Berlin 1945 in Augenzeugenberichten* (The Battle for Berlin, 1945, Based on Eyewitness Accounts) and Bengt von zur Mühlen's *Der Todeskampf der Reichshauptstadt* (The Death Throes of the Reich Capital), among others. In addition, some of the impressions I have cited come from information given to me by relatives and friends who lived through the last days of the German Reich.

Andreas-Friedrich, Ruth. *Schauplatz Berlin: Ein deutsches Tagebuch.* Munich: Rheinsberg Verlag G. Lentz, 1962. (*Battleground Berlin: Diaries, 1945–1948.* Translated by Anna Boerresen. New York: Paragon House, 1990.)

Bahnsen, Uwe, and James P. O'Donnell. *Die Katakombe: Das Ende in der Reichskanzlei.* Stuttgart, 1975.

Baur, Hans. *Ich flog Mächtige der Erde.* Kempten: A. Pröpster, 1956.

Below, Nicolaus von. *Als Hitlers Adjutant 1937–45.* Mainz, 1980. (*At Hitler's Side: The Memoirs of Hitler's Luftwaffe Adjutant 1937–1945.* Translated by Geoffrey Brooks. London: Greenhill Books/Mechanicsburg, PA: Stackpole Books, 2001.)

Boldt, Gerhardt. *Die letzten Tage der Reichskanzlei.* Zürich, 1947. (*Hitler: The Last Days.* Translated by Sandra Bance. New York: Coward McCann & Geoghegan, 1973.)

Bormann, Martin. *The Bormann Letters: The Private Correspondence between Martin Bormann and his Wife from January 1943 to April 1945.* Edited by H. R. Trevor-Roper. London, 1954.

———. *Le testament politique de Hitler.* Edited by H. R. Trevor-Roper. Paris, 1959. (*Testament of Adolf Hitler: the Hitler-Bormann Documents, February–April 1945.* Edited by François Genoud. Translated from the German by R. H. Stevens, with an introduction by H. R. Trevor-Roper. 1961.)

Bourke-White, Margaret. *"Dear Fatherland, Rest Quietly": A Report on the Collapse of Hitler's "Thousand Years."* New York: Simon and Schuster, 1946.

Boveri, Margaret. *Tage des Überlebens: Berlin 1945.* Munich: R. Piper, 1968.

Chuikov, Vasili I. (Tschuikow, Wassili I.). *Das Ende des Dritten Reiches.* [originally published in Russian] Munich, 1966.

Gosztony, Peter, ed. *Der Kampf um Berlin 1945 in Augenzeugenberichten.* Düsseldorf: Rauch, 1970.

Haffner, Sebastian. *Anmerkungen zu Hitler.* Munich: Kindler, 1978. (*The Meaning of Hitler.* Translated by Ewald Osers. Cambridge: Harvard University Press, 1978/1979.)

Joachimsthaler, Anton. *Hitlers Ende: Legenden und Dokumente.* Munich, 1999. (*The Last Days of Hitler: The Legends, the Evidence, the Truth.* Translated by Helmut Bögler. London: Arms & Armour Press, 1996.)

Kardorff, Ursula von. *Berliner Aufzeichnungen aus den Jahren 1942 bis 1945.* Munich: Biederstein, 1964. (*Diary of a Nightmare: Berlin, 1942–1945.* Translated by Ewan Butler. New York: John Day, 1966.)

Kempka, Erich. *Ich habe Adolf Hitler verbrannt.* Munich: Kyrburg, 1951.

Koller, Karl. *Der letzte Monat: Die Tagebuchaufzeichnungen des ehemaligen Chefs des Generalstabes der deutschen Luftwaffe vom 14. April bis zum 27. Mai 1945.* Mannheim: N. Wohlgemuth, 1949. (*Koller War Diary.* Edited by J. Richard Smith. Sturbridge, MA: Monogram Aviation Publications, 1990.)

Kuby, Erich. *Die Russen in Berlin 1945.* Munich, 1965. (*The Russians and Berlin, 1945.* Translated by A. J. Pomerans. New York: Hill and Wang, 1968.)

Müller, Rolf-Dieter, and Gerd R. Ueberschär. *Kriegsende 1945: Die Zerstörung des deutschen Reiches.* Frankfurt: Fischer Taschenbuch, 1994.

Musumanno, Michael A. *Ten Days to Die.* Garden City, N.Y.: Doubleday, 1950. (*In zehn Tagen kommt der Tod: Augenzeugen über das Ende Hitlers.* Munich, 1950.)

Reitsch, Hanna. *Fliegen, mein Leben.* Stuttgart, 1951.

Ruhl, Klaus-Jörg. *Deutschland 1945: Alltag zwischen Krieg und Frieden in Berichten, Dokumenten und Bildern.* Darmstadt/Neuwied: Luchterhand, 1984.

Ryan, Cornelius. *The Last Battle.* New York: Simon and Schuster, [1966] 1995. (*Der letzte Kampf.* Munich/Zurich, 1966.)

Schäfer, Hans Dieter. *Berlin im Zweiten Weltkrieg: Der Untergang der Reichshauptstadt in Augenzeugenberichten.* Munich: Piper, 1985.

Schenck, Ernst-Günther. *Ich sah Berlin sterben: Als Arzt in der Reichskanzlei.* Herford: Nicolaische Verlagsbuchhandlung, 1970.

Schroeder, Christa. *Er war mein Chef: Aus dem Nachlass der Sekretärin von Adolf Hitler.* Munich: Langen Müller, 1985.

Springer, Hildegard. *Es sprach Hans Fritzsche: Nach Gesprächen, Briefen und Dokumenten.* Stuttgart, 1949.

Steiner, Felix. *Die Armee der Geächteten.* Göttingen: Plesse Verlag, 1963.

Studnitz, Hans-Georg von. *While Berlin Burns: The Diary of Hans-Georg von Studnitz, 1943–1945.* Englewood Cliffs, NJ: Prentice-Hall, 1965. (*Als Berlin brannte: Diarium der Jahre 1943 bis 1945.* Stuttgart: W. Kohlhammer, 1963.)

Tissier, Tony le. *The Battle of Berlin 1945.* New York: St. Martin's Press, 1988. (*Der Kampf um Berlin 1945: Von den Seelower Höhen zur Reichskanzlei.* Frankfurt/Berlin, 1991.)

Toland, John. *The Last 100 Days.* New York: Random House, 1966. (*Das Finale: Die letzten hundert Tage.* Munich/Zurich, 1968.)

Trampe, Gustav, ed. *Die Stunde Null: Erinnerungen an Kriegsende und Neuanfang.* Stuttgart: Deutsche Verlagsanstalt, 1995.

Trevor-Roper, Hugh R. *The Last Days of Hitler.* London: Macmillan, 1971. (*Hitlers letzte Tage.* Berlin, 1965.)

Völklein, Ulrich, ed. *Hitlers Tod: Die letzten Tage im Führerbunker.* Göttingen: Steidl, 1998.

Zur Mühlen, Bengt von, ed. *Der Todeskampf der Reichshauptstadt.* Berlin: Chronos, 1994.

INDEX

ILLUSTRATION CREDITS

Grateful acknowledgement is made for permission to reproduce the following illustrations and maps:

pp. 57, 156–157: © Bildarchiv, Preussischer Kulturbesitz

pp. ii, 6, 7 right, 26, 98, 102, 113, 150–151, 161, 172: SV-Bilderdienst

p. 67: Bundesarchiv, Berlin

p. 170: Margaret Bourke-White/Time Pix

pp. 18, 50–51, 120: Keystone Germany

pp. 4, 7 left, 42, 59, 65, 91, 126, 138, 145, 168: Ullstein Bilderdienst

pp. 12, 15, 20: Peter Palm, Berlin/Germany